BATTLES WITHOUT BORDERS
The Rise and Fall of New France

By Bill Twatio

ESPRIT DE CORPS BOOKS
OTTAWA, CANADA

ACKNOWLEDGEMENTS

Misconceptions about the military history of Canada are compounded by the almost complete neglect of that history in the country's schools. There is a cherished national myth that as citizens of a peaceful country, we are unlikely or reluctant warriors. So prevalent is the myth that George F. Stanley, the dean of Canadian military historians subtitled his popular *Canada's Soldiers*, a survey of Canada's military past, "the military history of an unmilitary people." Canadians, even in this, the Year of the Veteran, no longer seem to be aware of how war has shaped the country.

Battles Without Borders is not a comprehensive military history of Canada, rather, it chronicles how war has defined our national identity from the first skirmishes between the Vikings and Dorset peoples, through the rise and fall of New France, the War of 1812, the rebellions in Upper and Lower Canada, to Confederation. How well it succeeds is for the reader to decide.

This book has been very much a collaborative effort. I would like to thank Katherine and Scott Taylor of *Esprit de Corps* for their patience with a sometimes cranky author, and Diana Rank and Darcy Knoll for their unfailing good humour in the face of a monumental editing task. I am particularly grateful to Julie Simoneau, without whose tireless efforts this book would not have been possible.

I am also grateful to Les Peate, who, drawing on his vast knowledge of early warfare and the British army, contributed the following pieces: "First Skirmishes," "Shamans, Warriors & Counting Coup," "Westward Ho! The British Arrive" and "A Soldier's Life is Awf'ly Hard."

Thank you all.

This book is dedicated to my mother, Rosemary Holland (1914-2004).

Contents

ALSO BY BILL TWATIO:

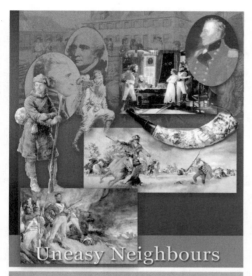

Far from being the "peaceful kingdom" of legend, inhabited by an "umilitary people," Canada has been shaped by war. Not only has war made the very existence of Canada possible, it also shaped our myths and memories, and defined our national identiry.

In *Uneasy Neighbours*, Bill Twatio chronicles the military history of Canada from the American Revolution and the War of 1812, to the rebellions in Upper and Lower Canada, the American Civil War, and the Fenian raids. Culminating with Confederation, *Uneasy Neighbours* describes how our country was forged in fire.

Other books published by Esprit de Corps Books:

The War That Wasn't tells the stories of the Canadians and their allies who served during the Korean War. *From Baddeck to the Yalu* brings to life the personal histories of the Canadian airmen who flew in the Great War, World War II and Korea.

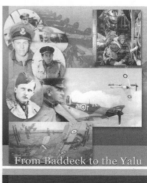

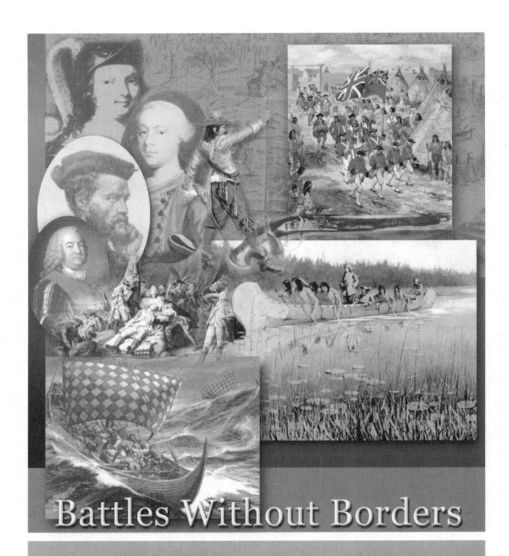

Battles Without Borders

The Rise and Fall of New France

BILL TWATIO

∂ THE FIRST SKIRMISHES

A thousand years ago the Vikings landed on the East Coast. Meeting a hostile reception from the Dorset native peoples, they curtailed their stay.

THERE IS A MISTAKEN tendency to attribute the beginning of Canada's military history to the French and Indian Wars of the mid-18th century. While these events certainly played a significant role in our military heritage and traditions, the Seven Years War (in which the North American battles, to many major participants, had little strategic value) were preceded by centuries of conflict in what is now Canada.

The original Canadian inhabitants included the Dorset, who had emigrated from Asia across a frozen Bering Strait between 8000 and 4000 B.C., and later made their way to what are now the Atlantic Provinces.

From the other direction, Vikings were moving westward. Eric the Red was outlawed for murder, and later led a group of Icelandic colonists to the barren island of Greenland. In 1001 A.D., a kinsman, Leif Eriksson visited

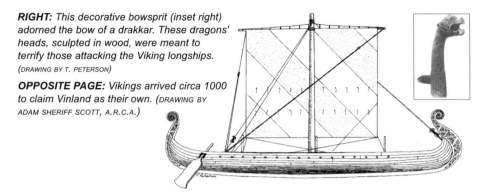

RIGHT: *This decorative bowsprit (inset right) adorned the bow of a drakkar. These dragons' heads, sculpted in wood, were meant to terrify those attacking the Viking longships.* (DRAWING BY T. PETERSON)

OPPOSITE PAGE: *Vikings arrived circa 1000 to claim Vinland as their own.* (DRAWING BY ADAM SHERIFF SCOTT, A.R.C.A.)

(and perhaps settled) areas in Labrador and a mysterious Vinland on the eastern coast, where his group wintered and returned to Greenland with produce and lumber from the New World. More colonization followed as growing and wildlife conditions were favourable, and the Vikings appeared set for a comfortable existence.

Eventually, the inevitable cultural clash occurred. In 1006 A.D. Thorvaldr Eriksson led a party of settlers into Vinland. During a reconnaissance for a new site, the Viking party encountered nine Dorset Indo-Inuit tribesmen (whom the Norsemen, with a sense of superiority over the natives that was not uncommon in later years, called skrellings meaning weaklings or barbarians in their language). Eight natives were killed; the ninth returned with reinforcements and assailed the Viking ship with arrows, mortally wounding the settlers' leader before being beaten off. Shortly after this incident, the Vikings decided that there was little future in settling the area, and left for good.

Although for the next five centuries North American native peoples were not bothered by European intrusion, theirs was not an altogether idyllic, peaceful existence. In the east, the Iroquois League tribes inhabited the area of the St. Lawrence River Valley and present-day New York State. The Iroquois, expert farmers, traded with the powerful Algonquin hunters who lived further north. However, over the years, warfare was common, often taking the form of raids on neighbouring settlements in search of wives, slaves, and booty.

Indeed, even within the Iroquois League and its allies, inter-tribal conflict was common and villages lived in a constant state of alert. The battles were no doubt minor clashes by European standards (sometimes a warrior would achieve status by "counting coup" – merely touching a foe in combat) and casualties were comparatively light as the major weapons used were knives, hatchets, spears and, to a lesser degree, bows and arrows. Nevertheless, at least four tribes, totalling over 40,000 people, were exterminated in wars during this period.

As an example of the brutality which sometimes occurred during these inter-tribal conflicts, early French explorers discovered a cave filled with the bodies of two hundred Micmac tribesmen, women and children who were burned alive by their enemies from another tribe. Unless they were useful as slaves, torture and death was the usual fate of prisoners.

At the turn of the 15th century, more Europeans arrived. Spanish, English, French, Portuguese and Dutch adventurers flocked to the New World. Giovanni Caboto (a.k.a. John Cabot) landed in Newfoundland (or, perhaps, Nova Scotia), in the service of Henry VII of England. He returned to England with tales of a land of plenty; later New Found Land became England's first overseas colony.

Other European nations were quick to explore and, often, settle the Americas. In the early years of the new century, some Aboriginals were captured or tricked into being taken to Europe, where, together with their artifacts, they became objects of wonder.

When Jacques Cartier arrived in Gaspé, he was greeted by Iroquois who, it would appear, had already been in contact with Europeans. At first, relations were friendly, and a lucrative exchange of gee-gaws for valuable furs was established. However, Cartier abused the hospitality of the Stadacona tribe by tricking or capturing their chief and his sons and taking them to France. Nevertheless, the Stadaconas continued to treat the French as friends.

While Cartier established a foothold in the Quebec area, English and Dutch settlers also begin establishing themselves on this new continent. The first settlers from Britain arrived in Newfoundland in 1588 (the year in which the Spanish Armada was defeated). Captain Martin Frobisher, whose objective was to mine gold in the Arctic areas and to find a Northwest Passage to the Far East, followed the fashion of seizing Inuit captives (all of whom died shortly after arriving in England).

Conflict was inevitable. In 1585 – as a foretaste of a conflict that still exists – the English destroyed a Spanish fishing settlement in Newfoundland. Meanwhile, the French had acquired a monopoly of the fur trade in New France, an area that included (what are now) Quebec and the Atlantic Provinces. French enclaves in the Bay of Fundy were attacked by British and Dutch colonists from further south. Not only was there international conflict, but often rival settlements would attack each other, especially in the interests of establishing trade for furs with the Aboriginals.

Samuel de Champlain, on his first visit to New France, attended a feast where his *Montagnais* allies celebrated the slaughter and scalping of 100 Iroquois foes. One notable escalation in tribal warfare occurred at Ticonderoga, where Champlain and 60 Hurons introduced firearms to the picture. Two Iroquois chiefs were felled with a single blast from the Frenchman's arquebus, and 200 Iroquois driven to flight. A few years later, in Ontario, Champlain was less fortunate, failing in an attempt to breach an Iroquois village with the aid of the Hurons.

Meanwhile, in Acadia (the New Brunswick region), an English expedition destroyed the French settlements. The issue was further complicated when both France and Britain later appointed governors for the undefined New World territories.

In the global picture, the colonization of North America was still a "sideshow." When war broke out again between Britain and France in 1627, the Kirke privateering family was authorized to displace the French from Canada. A number of vessels and settlements were captured, including the city of Quebec which was later returned to France after the Treaty of Saint-Germain-en-Laye was signed in 1632; Acadia also returned to French rule. Political considerations are not a new concept: the English monarch conceded these terms in order to obtain the balance of his dowry from his consort, the former Princess Henrietta of France. Privateer David Kirke was rewarded with the appointment of Governor of Newfoundland.

Meanwhile, the Europeans had introduced their native allies to European weapons. By mid-century, an estimated 500 Iroquois had firearms (most of them apparently supplied by the Dutch colonists in the Hudson River Valley), although their use in battle was perhaps more psychologically than militarily effective. Nevertheless, it was the start of what later became an arms race as the French, Dutch, English and later, American revolutionaries provided muskets and rifles to the Aboriginals, sometimes as "arms for

The search for the Northwest Passage lured many explorers, including Martin Frobisher. His 1577 expedition to Baffin Island quickly deteriorated, culminating in the Battle of Bloody Point. The Inuit he captured all died shortly after arriving in England. (WATERCOLOUR BY JOHN WHITE, BRITISH MUSEUM)

allies," but often as trade goods. Alliances between rival colonists and Indian tribes were established and frequently changed. The early sporadic tribal raids escalated – casualties frequently reaching four figures – and the Europeans would encourage their Indian allies to attack rival settlements.

In the 1650s, the British again became masters of Acadia. The French capital, Port Royal, was renamed Annapolis Royal. (Ironically, the force under Robert Sedgewick had originally intended to attack the New Netherlands, enemies in the First Anglo-Dutch War, but struck at Acadia in the interests of the fur traders.) The Treaty of Breda returned Acadia to France once again, but this time, Britain received Caribbean territory and the city of New Amsterdam (later New York) as spoils.

By now the Five Nations (the Iroquois), armed by and allied to the British, had become the most powerful tribal group in the region. Nevertheless, for the remainder of the century, combined French and Indian forces would continue to raid the New England and New York colonies.

Another significant development occurred in 1665. Until then, the fighting in North America had been carried out by the settlers and their native allies. While some of the leaders on both sides could claim military experience, regular troops were not employed. In 1665, following an appeal to France, the first of 1000 soldiers of the Régiment de Carignan-Salières disembarked at Quebec City (population 500), freshly blooded in a European war. They were followed by four companies of troops from the French West Indies. As their British enemies were soon to discover, tactics that served well on European battlefields were ineffective in the North Ameri-

Robert de La Salle sailed the first ship built and launched on the Great Lakes, the Griffon. Temperamental, suspicious, arrogant, and hated by his own men, de La Salle met his end in a swamp off the Gulf of Mexico in 1685, while trying to locate the mouth of the Mississippi.

can forests and, in their first major battle in 1666, they were soundly defeated by the Iroquois.

Another innovation in 1679 was the building and launching of the first sailing ship on the Great Lakes. The *Griffon*, although built by René-Robert Cavelier de La Salle for exploration and trading purposes, was equipped with seven cannons. A few years later another noted French explorer, Pierre Le Moyne, Sieur d'Iberville, took the conflict northwards with an expedition which seized the Hudson's Bay Company's forts on James Bay. One outcome of this incursion was the British decision to establish Fort Churchill to control the Hudson Bay area. Sadly, La Salle, an innovative and intrepid explorer and warrior, was murdered by his own men following a mutiny in the territory of Louisiana.

Meanwhile, Comte Louis de Buade de Frontenac, governor of New France, attempted to establish a compulsory militia embracing all adult male settlers. Although under-equipped and poorly trained, they did at least provide a fairly dependable source of manpower.

In 1690, Port Royal was again captured, this time by New England irregulars under Sir William Phips. Although the French were badly outnumbered, one significant element in the short action was the "combined operations" aspect, with the use of armed ships as well as land troops. A subsequent attempt to seize Quebec City was easily repulsed by Governor Frontenac since the British colonists' clumsy efforts were aggravated by a virulent outbreak of smallpox. Once more, what had been gained by force of arms was ceded by politicians. Under the 1697 Treaty of Ryswick, Port

Royal was again returned to France.

In the interim, the naval element entered the scene. The redoubtable Pierre Le Moyne, Sieur d'Iberville, took on three British ships in Hudson Bay with a single vessel, and sank two of them. His crews later captured the British post of York Factory.

Until the end of the 17th century, the conflicts in North America, despite their international implications, were more or less local affairs, aimed at preserving or increasing trade — especially in the lucrative fur commerce. Help and support from the home countries was negligible, although the French regular troops were later augmented by the Compagnies Franches de la Marine who were controlled by the Admiralty and Colonial departments. Apart from a handful of Dutch troops, no other regulars appeared until after the War of the Spanish Succession. (This 1700-1713 conflict was also known as Queen Anne's War.)

The main action in the 17th century was in Europe where formal territorial changes resulted from the treaties that ended those wars. Thus, despite their continuing warfare in Canada, France and England united to defeat the Dutch in Europe. As a result, in 1674, under the Treaty of Westminster, The Netherlands returned to Britain much of New York and New Jersey that had been seized the previous year. Not until the next century did the New World become a significant battleground in the struggle for world power.

LEFT: *John Cabot (Giovanni Caboto), was a Venetian explorer and navigator whose English-backed voyages were the basis of Britain's claim to Canada. On his voyage of 1497 he became the first known European to land in North America.*
(NEWFOUNDLAND ARCHIVES)

OPPOSITE PAGE: *Shamans were believed to possess special powers for healing, reading the future, and bringing about good hunting and fishing seasons.* (CANADIAN MUSEUM OF CIVILISATION)

SHAMANS, WARRIORS & COUNTING COUP

Although written records are lacking, there is evidence that warfare was a constant way of life in North America long before the arrival of the Europeans.

AN ABORIGINAL AMERICAN WAS bewildered by arrangements for commemorating Columbus Day in a nearby community. "What are you celebrating?" he asked. "Why, the discovery of America!" replied one of the townspeople. "What do you mean, DISCOVERY?" asked the irate Indian. "We'd never lost it!"

We tend to assume that Canada's military history began with the arrival of Europeans around 1500 A.D. In fact, warlike activities and strife had been very much a part of the aboriginal heritage for centuries before Jacques Cartier's arrival. The dearth of information of some of these vicious battles is partly due to lack of written records, so that most of our knowledge has to be pieced together from verbal accounts passed down through the generations or from archaeological research.

LEFT: *Iroquois warrior (circa 1795) armed with matchlock musket and axes. (ILLUSTRATION BY JACQUES GRASSET DE SAINT-SAUVEUR. NAC/c003163)*

BELOW: *Detail of the firing mechanism of an early matchlock flint rifle.*

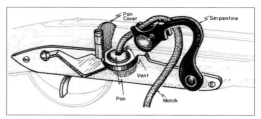

It is perhaps not surprising that accounts vary. Some sources describe major inter-tribal battles, creating casualties in the hundreds, while other accounts suggest that the warfare took the form of exchanged insults, the "counting coup," and the withdrawal of both sides when someone got hurt. Just as we cannot generalize on modern wars, with durations ranging from 40 minutes to 100 years, and casualties from nil to several million, neither can we stereotype the early inter-tribal conflicts.

Certainly, there are legends, many of them substantiated by subsequent archaeological finds, which indicate that warfare was fairly common among the many aboriginal groups in North America. From the early arrivals, who probably crossed from Asia via the Bering Strait "ice bridge" and moved southwards, to the Sioux and Cheyenne at Little Big Horn, there are many accounts. While much of what is now Canada's history was, of necessity, tied to that of our southern neighbours (Indian tribes knew or cared little for artificial national European-established boundaries), there are striking similarities across the continent. From the West Coast Haida, whose canoe-borne raids struck terror into the hearts of their neighbours, through the Blackfoot and Cree of the Plains who lived in an almost perpetual state of war, to the Micmac who considered fighting proficiency the way to prestige in their tribe, and the now-extinct Dorset (who drove off their Viking invaders with their fearsome "secret weapon"), conduct of war had much in common.

RIGHT: *Used since 8000 B.C., the atlatl was a two- to three-foot piece of wood with a small base carved in its butt end. The spear rested on the upper face of the atlatl and was held in place by the base and hand.*

Generally, *casi belli* were more straightforward than in the Asian-European world. While territorial claims were somewhat nebulous, the general aim of aggressors was often to obtain slaves or steal food stocks. In some tribes, warfare was the road to prestige for males with leadership aspirations. Elite "warrior societies" existed, perhaps the most dreaded of which was the Kootenay "Crazy Dogs," an earlier "SS-type" force. Revenge and retaliation for past raids might set tribes on the warpath. A state of war or tension could exist for centuries between hereditary enemies, with short periods of actual fighting punctuating an uneasy state of constant alert.

Conduct of war was, by European standards, unsophisticated. Despite Hollywood's graphic portrayals of thousands of screaming braves overwhelming the "good guys," usually only a small percentage of tribal males were actually mobilized for war. In *War Before Civilization*, Lawrence Keeley compares the 5 to 10 per cent of tribal males from Huron and Iroquois tribes who went into combat with the figures for 20th century wars, when almost half of the French male population was called to the Colours. This is of course partly offset by the fact that most native warriors served as "sharp end" fighters. (In many cases, the administrative "tail" of supply carriers and "first-aiders" to the injured was limited and provided by female band members.)

Periods of hostility were generally of short duration. The need for food necessitated the presence of the warriors as hunters or fishermen, while

LEFT: *Inter-tribal warfare was not usually related to territory, but to a warrior's prestige in a tribe or to obtain food or slaves. (NAC/c92245)*

RIGHT: *Coup sticks were sometimes decorated with the images of tribal enemies.*

seasonal conditions restricted mobility, and limited means of transporting food and supplies precluded long campaigns. Pitched battles were less common than raids or ambushes against other settlements. One British Columbia tribe habitually attacked isolated villages or camps in hard winters, killing off the inhabitants and living off their food stocks.

Leadership was more of the "follow me" school than disciplined command and control. One important factor was the limited effectiveness of "missile" weapons, which meant that most battles consisted of close-quarter melees.

The bow and arrow was seldom lethal over about a hundred yards. While it was considerably more accurate than the first muskets encountered by the Aboriginals, and had a far higher rate of fire, use of shields and armour reduced its effects. A heavier projectile, the spear, was deadly within about 50 yards or more if an ingenious device — the atlatl — was used. This was a wooden contraption that was, in effect, an extension of a spear thrower's arm, and added significantly to the range and accuracy of the projectile. Some warrior bands used slingshots, and both sides might throw stones and rocks at their foes (one task of the female "auxiliaries" was to collect enemy missiles so that their fighters could return them against the foe). Early biological warfare in some cases was carried out by dipping arrow- or spearheads in toxic substances, usually snake venom or the rotting entrails of dead animals.

It was, however, the close-quarter melees that forced the outcome of the battle. While the missile weapons may have disrupted the enemy line, and perhaps even created a few casualties, the hand-to-hand combat usually decided the day. Here the weapons used were axes (before the arrival of the Europeans and their more sophisticated iron tomahawks, usually made of stone) as well as flint knives and a variety of wood and stone war clubs.

In some tribes, especially among the Plains Indians, the aim of aspiring warriors was not necessarily to kill their foes, but to "count coup" by touching an enemy either by hand or with a special "coup stick." Counting coup was sometimes recognized by the award of an eagle feather, worn in the hero's head-dress much as in modern days bravery is rewarded by medals and ribbons. "Bonus points" could be attained by killing and scalping the enemy.

While many groups despised body protection, shields and armour were used at times. One of the effects of bombarding the enemy with spears and other missiles was to cause the defenders to use their shields as protection against them, thus enabling the attackers to rush their enemy while the shields were ineffective against close-quarter attack. Some tribes adopted a form of wooden armour, consisting of slats or sticks bound in the form of a venetian blind, which was worn as a breastplate. One northwestern warrior, probably legendary, supposedly went to battle clad in a suit of armour made from bearskin, reinforced by "tiles" of copper, which was virtually the only metal used by North American natives before the arrival of the Europeans. Some Aleutian and Inuit warriors may have worn "armour" of multi-layered sealskin. Shields were usually made of animal skins, and, in some cases, were supposedly endowed with a mystical form of protection for the bearer.

Logistics were basic. Field rations of dried meat, corn, berries or fish would be carried by the warrior — usually about four days' supply. Women or slaves could be conscripted to bear additional supplies. Transportation was usually on foot (horses were not introduced until the 16th century) or by canoe. The frail birchbark or skin canoes used by the riverine tribes were often vulnerable to destruction by enemies. In the northwest, sturdier dugout war canoes were employed, and the Haida, in particular, created terror when their vessels appeared, bearing ferocious raiders wearing frightening war-helmets.

Mystical support was provided by a tribal shaman, a religious leader, whose function in battle would today probably consist of a combination of chaplain, political commissar and medic. ("First aid" often consisted of the removal of the arrowhead and sucking the blood from the wound, a chancy business if poisoned arrows had been used.) Some tribes had four leaders; whose authority depended on the situation. There were the tribal heads, who supervised everyday activities as well as acting as political leaders, the war chiefs who commanded military operations; spiritual aid was invoked by the shaman or medicine man; and, in some cases, a ceremonial chief was the authority on ritual matters.

There was no Geneva Convention in pre-Columbian North America. Enemies who were wounded or unable to escape capture were usually despatched on the scene. Sometimes captives would be taken to the victors' villages. If they were lucky, and the acquisition of slaves was one of the victors' objectives, they would be adopted into the tribe to replace braves who had died earlier. They would often be accepted as full members of the group, and, in time, would be completely assimilated, even to the extent of being recruited as members of war parties against their own people. Women and children seized on raids would also be "adopted."

Others were less fortunate. In some areas, captives had to "run the gauntlet" between two rows of warriors, wives and children who would lash out at them with clubs, sticks and fists. Those who survived might be accepted into their captors' society; those who didn't suffered a terrible fate and could be turned over to the ladies for exquisite forms of torture. It was a matter of pride that these victims would remain stoical throughout their ordeal. (In some tribes, the captives were expected to chant songs of defiance until their tongues were finally silenced by a merciful death.) Often parts of the bodies would be eaten, especially in the case of particularly brave victims. Devouring vital organs, such as the heart and liver, would supposedly transfer the heroic qualities to the eater.

Scalping of victims was not widespread until after the arrival of the Europeans, who often put a bounty on the scalps of their enemies. Archaeological discoveries indicate that some victims were scalped in earlier days and the scalps (and, in some cases, entire heads) displayed as trophies.

Many communities established defensive works in the form of ditches and palisades. While they provided some protection, a determined enemy could often overcome them. One significant discovery occurred at Crow Creek, in South Dakota, where the remains of 500 casualties of a 14th century massacre were found. The victims, of all age groups and both sexes, had been clubbed or speared to death. Evidence of malnutrition in the remains suggests that the massacre was generated by a food raid by neighbouring villagers. According to tribal lore, the Crow Creek incident was the last of the major battles between the Sioux and Arikara tribes, which suggests that such raids were not uncommon.

Overall, it is perhaps to safe to say that despite the efforts required for sheer survival, necessity or less creditable reasons forced a constant state of hot or cold war among Canada's first peoples. Though not as well documented as later conflicts, they are, indeed, a part of our national military heritage.

The people of the Dorset culture were the descendants of Siberian immigrants, who were the first occupants of Arctic North America. They lived in the Arctic for over three millenia, developing a unique way of life in apparent isolation from other human groups. This life-sized mask was carved from driftwood and painted; it originally had fur moustaches and eyebrows attached with pegs. Shamans probably wore the masks in rituals for curing the sick, controlling the weather, or influencing the hunt. (CMC/ PFFM-1:1728)

THE MARINER OF ST. MALO

A minor nobleman who had seen better days, Jacques Cartier claims a new land for the King of France in 1534

LEGEND HAS IT THAT, as an old man, he was a congenial tippler who haunted the taverns of his native St. Malo regaling the patrons with tall tales. And what tales Jacques Cartier had to tell! Tales of a great river, strange people and gold, silver and jewels in the fabulous Kingdom of the Saguenay.

He was in his mid-forties, a minor nobleman who had seen better days when, in April 1534, he set sail from St. Malo bearing instructions from François I, the King of France, to discover "certain isles and countries where, it is said, there must be great quantities of gold and other riches." Cartier also believed that he might find the fabled Northwest Passage to Cathay and the Spice Islands.

Fair winds swiftly carried his ships across the northern seas, but his heart sank when he sailed through the Strait of Belle Isle and sighted Labrador.

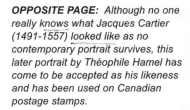

RIGHT: *Cartier stands at the base of the cross he erected at Gaspé in 1534, claiming the land for the King of France. He assured the curious Iroquois that it was only a landmark.* (PAC)

"I did not see one cartload of earth," he wrote. "I believe that this was the land God gave to Cain." He also made contact with the native people whom he dismissed as "the sorriest folk there can be in the world." With provisions running low, he headed south into the Baie de Gaspé, where on July 14, 1534 he erected a 30-foot cross embellished with the fleur-de-lys and the slogan "Long live the King of France!" claiming the land in the name of François I. Disingenuously, he assured a local chief that it was only a landmark for vessels that might come that way. Late in the season, convinced that the wide estuary he had entered was the long-sought passage to Cathay, he sailed for home with two natives he had taken captive.

The following year, aboard the *Grande Hermine*, he sailed past Anticosti Island into the St. Lawrence and proceeded upstream to the Iroquois settlement of Stadacona beneath the rock of Quebec City. Warmly welcomed by the chief, Donnacona, he left his larger ships behind and moved on to Hochelaga. Climbing a mountain he named in honour of the bishop of Monreale in Sicily, he looked over "the finest land it is possible to see."

Cartier wintered along the Saint-Charles River, near Stadacona. His ships and huts were coated with ice and the river froze to a depth of 12 feet. Scurvy struck and 25 of his men died before the Indians showed him how to brew a remedy from the bark and leaves of the white cedar. In the spring, as the expedition prepared to return to France, he invited Donnacona and others to a farewell ceremony and took them prisoner.

Cartier would not return for another five years and, by then, Donnacona and his companions were dead. Few of the Iroquois at Stadacona believed his story that they were living in luxury in France. The new chief, Agona, was hostile, he and his people sensing that Cartier had come to stay. He had. This time, his expedition included stonemasons, carpenters, farmers, and 700 soldiers armed with arquebuses, crossbows, and artillery. Bedecked in black and white livery, they wore the first uniforms seen in Canada.

The expedition was under the command of Jean-François de La Rocque, Sieur de Roberval, a nobleman and soldier and intimate of the King. Cartier was the junior commander because of his lack of military experience and inferior social position. Building a fort at what he called Charlesbourg-Royal (now Quebec City), eight miles above Stadacona, he endured the winter of 1542 besieged by the embittered Iroquois. His soldiers occupied themselves by gathering "precious stones." In June, with twelve barrels of treasure aboard, he sailed for France.

As Cartier's ships headed home, Roberval and 200 settlers were en route to Charlesbourg-Royal. They met in Newfoundland. But Cartier had no intention of lingering in the land God gave to Cain. Disobeying orders to return to the settlement, he slipped away into a fog bank bound for St. Malo. After five months of incredible misery at Cap Rouge, Roberval also returned to France as quickly as he could.

Cartier was soon a bitterly disappointed man. The King of France, François I, would never again confer the command of an expedition upon him and the treasure he had carried home was nothing but worthless rock (fool's gold). He did, however, enrich the French language. From then on, anyone wanting to convey the idea of utter worthlessness had only to refer to a Canadian diamond: "Voilà, un diamant du Canada."

RIGHT: *In 1541, Cartier built a fort at Charlesbourg-Royal (later to become Port Royal), but returned to France the following summer. (ILLUSTRATION BY C.W. JEFFERYS)*

OPPOSITE PAGE: *This illustration exaggerates the number of beavers to be found in Canada; but the demand for beaver fur in French fashion drove the economy of this developing land. (PAC/NMC - 26825)*

੨ THE FUR TRADE

The humble beaver and the growing
popularity of fur in Europe laid the basis
for the economy of New France.

THROUGHOUT THE MIDDLE AGES, fur was a status symbol worn almost exclusively by the nobility, sometimes as a badge of office. Judges wore ermine, great lords sable; and, in some places, its use was regulated by law. Nobles could wear furs prescribed for their various ranks; commoners could not wear them at all.

Most furs were rare and expensive and came from the forests of Russia, Poland and Scandinavia. The only fur in common use was beaver, made into felt for the hat trade. Hatters on the continent were using fur felt in the mid-16th century. It was first used in England in 1510 and became so popular that, a few years later, "beaver" became a synonym for hat.

With beaver in demand, settlers in North America began to exchange cheap cloth and cheaper hardware for pelts. Beaver was the fur-bearing animal most hunted by the northern Indians, for its meat as well as its fur.

Early settlers, like Cartier (standing right), established trade with local tribes. Cartier dismissed the fur trade as "a thing of small profit." (THE ROBERT SIMPSON COMPANY)

Beaver robes — five to eight furs sewn together — were their preferred winter garments.

The first traders often bartered for furs off the Indians' backs. Such furs were prized because, before sewing them into robes, the Indians scraped the underside of each skin to loosen the roots of the guard hairs. Most fell out and, as the robes were worn fur side in, the remaining guard hairs were rubbed off, exposing the soft undercoat. In time, the Basques, followed by the English, French and Dutch, began taking trade goods on their whaling and fishing expeditions, and disposed of the pelts they acquired at a handsome profit.

Jacques Cartier had described the North American fur trade as "a thing of small profit." Forty years after his last voyage, his home port of St. Malo was fitting out expeditions for the fur trade alone, and a collection of furs at Paris was valued at twenty thousand crowns. By 1600, the French were trading needles, awls, knives, hatchets and cooking pots to the Indians along the St. Lawrence, and were making arrowheads of iron especially for the northern tribes.

Better armed and anxious to maintain a monopoly on the trade, the Montagnais, Micmac, and Algonquin drove the Iroquois out of the St. Lawrence Valley by the end of the century.

In the next century, the popularity of the beaver hat led to a phenomenal expansion of the fur trade. One of the early Jesuit priests reported that up to 20 trading ships called annually at Tadoussac, the post at the mouth of the Saguenay River, taking 22,000 pelts in one year. Lynx, fox, otter, muskrat, and marten were added gradually as the market for these dressed furs grew with the rise of the middle class, and traders, businessmen and commoners began aping the fashions of the nobility.

Beaver was plentiful in North America, numbering some 60 million, and relatively easy to catch. The best beaver pelts were taken in winter when the fur was thickest, and the animals were confined to their lodges. Before steel traps came into use in 1797, various techniques were used. Some hunters built dead falls in which an animal trying to take bait triggered a device that dropped a log on its neck. Others cut holes in the ice to attract beaver and put them within reach. At other times of the year, earth was dropped through a lodge's air vent to stampede the beaver into underwater nets, or dams were broken to drain the deep ponds in which beaver could hide.

New France was the only colony founded on the fur trade, but the English in Virginia and the Dutch along the Hudson River also traded for furs. Most pelts came from the Canadian Shield and were traded from tribe to tribe. A great class of Indian middlemen arose among the Huron and Iroquois, tribes that did little trapping themselves but travelled far, trading their corn, beans, squash, and tobacco for the pelts collected by the hunting tribes. The Huron were the most successful because they remained at peace with the tribes north of the St. Lawrence, the traditional enemies of the Iroquois.

Until the arrival of the white man, tribal warfare was little more than a kind of savage sport, conducted with elaborate ritual. The object was to win glory, take scalps, capture a few prisoners to be tortured, and, if they proved to be very brave, to be eaten as a means of acquiring their courage. Under the influence of the fur traders, however, Indian rivalries turned into deadly wars of attrition.

By the late 1600s, nearly 100,000 beaver pelts were being traded each year, and traders were making up to two thousand percent profit. Nobody bothered to tell the Indians.

Exposed to the elements and the hardships of the Canadian wilderness, trappers and coureurs de bois led the way. (PUBLIC ARCHIVES OF CANADA)

ぬ THE FUTURE OF NEW FRANCE

At the beginning of the 17th century, Canada was colonized and alliances formed with the tribes. Enemies were made too. For the first time, the natives encountered firearms.

AFTER JACQUES CARTIER'S failure to establish a settlement, the French did not return to Canada for more than 50 years. In 1604, Sieur de Monts built a fort at Port Royal on the Bay of Fundy and, four years later, dispatched an expedition led by Samuel de Champlain to the site of Quebec City, convinced that it lay on the route to Cathay "whence great riches could be drawn." Here, on 3 July 1608, Champlain began work on the Habitation, the first permanent settlement in New France.

Sickness and hunger claimed all but eight of the settlers that first dreadful winter, before ships arrived from France with supplies and reinforcements. To ensure the colony's survival, Champlain quickly realized that the fur trade must be developed, and that he would need allies. And so, in the

RIGHT: *Engraving depicting one of the first skirmishes between Champlain and the Iroquois at Ticonderoga near Lake Champlain, in 1609. (NATIONAL LIBRARY OF CANADA/ NL-6643)*

OPPOSITE PAGE: *Although no authentic portrait of Champlain is known to exist, we do know that he was thin and wiry, and below-average height.*

summer of 1609, he pledged his support to the neighbouring Algonquin and Huron tribes against the Iroquois Confederacy and set off with a war party into the wilderness. In doing so, he set the stage for a century of conflict.

Plagued by blackflies and mosquitoes, he moved south along the Richelieu, "the River of the Iroquois," into the lake that now bears his name. As he approached a promontory on the western shore, he encountered a war party of Mohawk. Armed with an arquebus, Champlain took up a battle position and waited.

"They came slowly to meet us and at their head were three chiefs," he recounted in his journal. "Our Indians likewise advanced and told me that those who had the three big plumes were the chiefs, and that I was to kill them. My white companions went unnoticed into the woods. Our Indians divided into two groups and put me ahead some 20 yards and I marched on until I was within some 30 yards of the enemy, who as soon as they caught sight of me halted and gazed at me and I at them. When I saw them make a move to draw their bows upon us, I took aim with my arquebus and shot straight at one of the three chiefs, and with this shot two fell to the ground, and one of their companions was wounded. This frightened the enemy greatly. One of my companions fired a shot from within the woods, which astonished them again so much that, seeing their chief dead, they lost courage and took to flight. I pursued them and laid low still more of them."

This brief encounter had tremendous consequences. Although it raised Champlain's prestige among his allies, he had aroused the fury of a terrible enemy. From then on, the mighty Confederacy of the Five Nations, embracing the Mohawk, Oneida, Onondaga, Cayuga, and Seneca, was the deadly foe of the French, and New France would pay the price in blood and terror.

In the years to come, Champlain would travel throughout the Huron country and take part in new battles with the Iroquois. In 1618, his explorations at an end, he settled down to nurse his feeble little colony at Quebec. He built roads and new fortifications, established an island fort upriver at Deschambault, and started another habitation at Trois-Rivières. Encouraged as new settlers arrived, he urged them "to cultivate the land before all things." Most, however, were bent on enriching themselves as quickly as possible and returning to France. He smoothed out quarrels among the tribes and unsuccessfully sought peace with the Iroquois.

In 1628, he learned that Cardinal Richelieu, first minister to the King, had formed the Company of One Hundred Associates and declared that 300 colonists would be sent to Quebec each year. It was news that Champlain had yearned to hear, but it had come too late. In July 1629, he was forced to surrender his beloved settlement to David Kirke, the rapacious commander of an expedition from the English colonies to the south, and sailed for England as a prisoner.

It was not until 1633 that Champlain returned to Quebec City to begin the work of rebuilding. He died on Christmas Day, 1635, when the population of the colony numbered barely 200 men, women and children. But his colony had taken root. It would survive and his legend as the Father of New France would grow with it.

"No other colony in America," historian Samuel Eliot Morison wrote, "is so much the lengthened shadow of one man as Canada is of the valiant, wise and virtuous Samuel de Champlain."

LEFT: *This map of New France, by Samuel de Champlain, published in 1632, three years before his death, is remarkably accurate. The essential geography of Canada – from Newfoundland to the Great Lakes – was charted mostly by Champlain himself.* (PAC/NMC 15661)

OPPOSITE PAGE: *French soldiers of the early 17th century armed with arquebuses. The matchlock musket was balanced on a forked rest before firing.* (BROWN MILITARY COLLECTION)

🕭 CHAMPLAIN'S ARQUEBUS

Although early firearms gave Europeans an advantage over the Indians in the 17th and 18th centuries, the bow was much more deadly.

KNOWN TO THE INDIANS as the *Thunderhorn*, Champlain's arquebus was actually a matchlock musket. It was a long, cumbersome, smoothbore weapon averaging about .80 calibre, which had to be balanced on a forked rest in order to take proper aim. It was fired by a lock on which a serpentine held a match or wick that had to be kept glowing and adjusted to ignite the powder in the pan. It was loaded by pouring a measured amount of powder down the barrel and pushing a ball of lead on top of it with a ramrod. A small amount of powder was then put into the pan to insure ignition of the main charge. Loading required no fewer than 23 separate movements.

The arquebus gave Champlain an advantage over the Indians, but not much. In every competition in Europe between crossbows, bows and arrows, and firearms until the end of the sixteenth century, the bow emerged victorious, usually by a score of something in the order of 20 to 16. But bows gradually fell out of favour, largely because they just could not match the range of the musket or shoulder-firearm.

Other types of firearms were available from the gunsmiths of Europe in Champlain's time, but they were too expensive for military use. The most common was the wheel-lock pistol, invented in Italy towards the end of the 15th century. It worked on the same principle as the modern cigarette lighter in which the spark is produced by scraping the serrated edge of a wheel against a piece of stone, in this case, pyrites.

Champlain eventually had both types of musket in his arsenal. A list of goods left behind at Quebec City when the Habitation was captured by the Kirkes in 1629, included "fourteen matchlock muskets; one wheel-lock arquebus; two large wheel arquebuses from six to seven feet long; two others of the same length, firing by match." The Kirkes' were armed with 75 muskets, 25 fowling pieces and 30 pistols.

The flintlock musket emerged as the universal favourite, probably because flint was cheap, readily available and more reliable. The mechanism was relatively simple. A small piece of spark-producing flint was held in the vice-like jaws of the cock, which was activated by a 'V' spring, so that when the trigger was pulled, the flint moved rapidly forward to strike the steel frizzen, or hammer. The force of the flint hitting the frizzen lifted it and the pan cover up allowing the sparks to fall into the pan igniting the charge. It could be fired in damp weather or in a light rain.

A flintlock was about five and a half feet in length, with a bore of approximately three-quarters of an inch. Because the bore was smooth, its accuracy was lamentable. A flintlock would rarely hit a standing target at more than 50 or 60 yards, while, to shoot at anything still visible at 100 yards, was simply a waste of ammunition. The bullet weighed about an ounce and fit loosely into the barrel to prevent fouling the powder. The powder created a thick black smoke, which came to be known as "the fog of war."

Between 1720 and 1730, the British musket took on a form which was to change very little in the next 80 years, and it came to be affectionately known as the Brown Bess. Loading required many motions. First a soldier had to remove a paper cartridge containing powder and ball from a box at his hip. Next, he tore open the cartridge with his teeth, sprinkling a few grains of gunpowder into the firing pan, ramming some of the paper down the barrel with a ramrod, followed by the rest of the powder, the wadded cartridge and the ball.

At best, a good soldier could fire the Brown Bess twice a minute, but even this frequency could not be maintained if a bayonet was plugged into the muzzle. Occasionally, in the heat of battle, soldiers would load powder and ball without ramming. The untamped charge would fall harmlessly to the ground within 30 yards. Most officers frowned on attempted rapid fire. "There is no need for firing fast," General James Wolfe told his troops. "A cool, well-levelled fire with the pieces carefully loaded is more destructive and formidable than the quickest fire in confusion."

It would be about two centuries before a shoulder-firearm firing a single bullet at a time became obsolete, succeeded by the amazingly accurate long-range rifle, so called because armament manufacture had become a German monopoly and the German word *rifeln* meant, to groove. Usually, four spiral grooves were machined into the bore of a rifle that seized the bullet, giving it a rapid spin that vastly increased both its accuracy and range. Later, rifles were equipped with chambers holding clips of from five to eight bullets, making it a formidable weapon.

Champlain would have been amazed.

Matchlock musket mechanism, 1630. Towards the end of the sixteenth century, portable firearms were becoming more common. The crossbow was replaced by the musket and the arquebus, heavy, solid firearms that were charged with round stone or lead bullets. A match or, later, a flint, activated by a wheel mechanism, ignited the powder. (MUSÉE DE L'ARMÉ, PARIS, FRANCE/CANADIAN MUSEUM OF CIVILIZATION/CMC S2004-648)

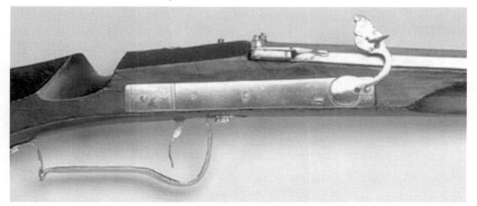

∝ THE FIRST FALL OF QUEBEC, 1629

Champlain's dreams for his beloved colony are set aside in exile and despair.

BY 1620, SAMUEL DE CHAMPLAIN'S roving and sea-faring days were over and he had settled down to nurture his little colony beneath the Rock at Quebec City. But the colony was little more than a trading post racked by internal rivalries. Louis Hébert, the only person seriously trying to farm, was being harassed as an enemy of the fur trade, liquor and fire-arms were being sold to the Indians, and the Habitation lay in ruins. Years after its founding, the colony had fewer than 70 permanent residents.

With characteristic energy Champlain set to work cleaning and repairing buildings and, when that was done, began to build a wooden fort on Cape Diamond called Fort Saint-Louis. He persuaded friendly Indians to settle near Quebec City and till the soil, smoothed out quarrels among the trad-ers and tribes, and unsuccessfully sought peace with the Iroquois. He built roads and supervised the construction of a settlement downriver at Cap Tourmente for the raising of cattle and hay. And in 1624, he built a new

RIGHT: *Champlain travelled extensively during his first 15 years in Canada, mapping most of the uncharted land from Newfoundland to the Great Lakes. (C.W. JEFFERYS)*

OPPOSITE PAGE: *Champlain leaving Quebec City after the victory of the Kirke brothers. However, the loss of the city was only temporary, since the Treaty of Saint-Germain-en-Laye returned the colony to France in 1632. (ILLUSTRATION BY C.W. JEFFERYS)*

stone Habitation on low ground facing the St. Lawrence.

Champlain had dreams for the colony. In 1618 he had proposed to Louis XIII and the Paris Chamber of Commerce that the city of Quebec be developed as a large fortified community. The St. Lawrence, he argued, was the shortest route to "the Kingdom of China and the East Indies, whence great riches could be drawn." He believed that customs duties on goods passing to and from the Orient would far surpass those collected in France. With the King's support, he returned to Canada as lieutenant to the Duc de Montmorency in 1620, this time with his wife Hélène.

As always, the fate of the colony depended on events in Europe. In March 1627, King Charles I of England declared war on France, motivated in part by his desire to help the persecuted French Huguenots. For English merchants, however, the war provided an opportunity to wrest the colony and the profitable fur trade away from France. In 1628, they formed the Company of Merchant Adventurers in Canada and began to outfit an expeditionary force.

Prime movers behind the establishment of the Adventurers were Gervase Kirke, a merchant of London and Dieppe and his five sons: David, Lewis, Thomas, John and James. Provided with letters of marque from the King, they set sail for Quebec aboard three ships in March 1628, with David in command.

Rounding the Gaspé peninsula, Kirke captured a French supply ship and several Basque fishing boats. At Tadoussac he landed a shore party to raze the settlement at Cap Tourmente, then sent messengers on to Quebec City demanding its surrender. Facing starvation, and with only a few barrels of biscuits and beans in store, Champlain brazenly replied that he had soldiers and plenty of food and "were we to surrender...we should not be worthy of the name of men in the presence of our King." He took heart, knowing that supply ships under the command of Claude Rougemont de Brison were on their way from France.

On the night of July 17, Rougemont tried to steal past the English ships under cover of fog. At daybreak Kirke sighted him below Tadoussac and opened fire. After a furious cannonade, Rougemont struck his colours and asked for terms. Plundering his ships of a staggering 165,000 pounds of goods, Kirke allowed him to return to France to face angry shareholders of his parent company, the Hundred Associates. "He was more brave than wise," Champlain said, noting that he should have stayed in the Bay of Gaspé until assured that the Kirkes were well out into the Gulf.

David Kirke had captured a fortune, but missed the opportunity to take Quebec. That triumph would have to wait.

Back in London, the Kirkes and William Alexander Jr., whose father held the fief to Nova Scotia, formed the Anglo-Scotch Company. Their ambitions knew no bounds. Not only did they plan to take Quebec, they now intended to rule all of Canada, planting Scotch colonies in Acadia and Cape Breton Island. In the spring of 1629, Alexander landed at the then-deserted French settlement at Port Royal with two shiploads of soldiers and settlers and set to work building Fort Charles. At the same time, the Kirkes set sail for Quebec and James Stewart, Lord Ochiltree and 60 more Scottish settlers came ashore on Cape Breton Island to build Fort Rosmar on the site of what would become the fortress of Louisbourg.

At Quebec, the situation was now desperate. His supplies exhausted, Champlain was forced to send men into the forests to gather acorns and roots. Neighbouring Indians spared some food and fish was plentiful in the river, but only eels could be taken because of the lack of nets, lines and hooks.

Anchoring off Tadoussac, Kirke captured a French relief ship then sent his brothers, Lewis and Thomas, ahead to Quebec to demand Champlain's surrender. Taking shelter behind Pointe Lévis, they went ashore under a white flag concealing the fact that England and France were now at peace, having signed the Treaty of Susa on April 24. Aware that his relief ship had been taken and that he could hold out no longer, Champlain capitulated. The only food left was small quantities of peas and Indian corn, a few acorns and 1,200 eels.

As a dejected Champlain and his colonists boarded the Kirkes' ships at Quebec, a French fleet was approaching Cape Breton Island. Learning that the English were in Quebec, they turned back after attacking the Scots at Fort Rosmar and evacuating the garrison. The Kirkes, not anxious to share their fate, left a strong force behind at Quebec with plenty of supplies before they packed up their prisoners for the journey back to England. Of the French, only the widow of Louis Hébert, her children and grandchildren, and one other family remained behind.

Champlain and the first prisoners reached Tadoussac on August 1, where he was enraged to learn that his protégés, Etienne Brûlé and Nicolas Marsolet had defected to the English and served as guides for the Kirkes. Champlain reached Dover on October 29, loudly protesting the capture of Quebec in peacetime, and demanding its immediate return. The Kirkes, French citizens, he considered traitors beneath contempt. Paroled, he took his case to the French court, beseeching the King and Cardinal Richelieu not to forsake his colony. Once again, he extolled its potential and, speaking from bitter experience, said that, in the future, there should be an obligation "to cultivate the land, before all things, in order to have the basic foodstuffs on the spot." Finally, in 1632, the colony was returned to France under the terms of the Treaty of Saint-Germain-en-Laye, Charles I of England giving it and Acadia up in return for an overdue payment on his wife's dowry. The Kirkes and the merchants of London lost every shilling they had invested in their effort to add Canada to the King's overseas possessions.

It was 1633 before Champlain returned to Quebec as the undisputed master of New France. Certain that he would never see France again, he had left all his possessions behind with his wife. Cannons boomed from the dilapidated citadel as he stepped ashore. The Héberts were on hand to greet him, and an Indian chief lamented in a formal oration that "while you were away the earth was no longer the earth, the river was no longer the river, the sky was no longer the sky." He was an old man now, and, perhaps suspecting that his time was short, immersed himself in his work in what were to be the happiest years of his life.

Once again, he rebuilt the Habitation, then enlarged the fortification and constructed an island fort upriver at Deschambault. Starting a new Habitation at Trois-Rivières, he felt "new courage" as more and more settlers arrived. He willingly granted commissions to anyone willing to explore the west As a token of gratitude for the restoration of the colony, he erected the chapel of Notre Dame de la Recouvrance on the site of the present-day Basilica. Although the Iroquois threat was worse than ever, he was optimistic. He treated his Indian allies as equals and they revered him. "Our sons will wed your daughters," he told them, "and henceforth we shall be one people."

He began to plan campaigns against the English and the Dutch on Manhattan Island, who were becoming active rivals in the fur trade. The last letter to Richelieu was a request for 120 soldiers to defend the colony and the Great Lakes.

In October 1635, he suffered a stroke and was put to bed in the citadel he had built. He died on Christmas Day and was buried with all the pomp and circumstance the little colony could command. And the following year when the Hurons came down to trade, they brought presents to help the French "wipe away their tears."

LEFT: *Established in 1600, Tadoussac was the first trading post built for the bartering of furs between French and Indian traders. For 200 years, it remained a key trading post and missionary centre. It was also the sight of several key events, including Rougemont's surrender to the Kirkes.*

OPPOSITE PAGE: *In the summer of 1615, Étienne Brûlé was dispatched to Lake Erie to enlist the aid of the Susquehanna. During this expedition, he travelled along the Humber River, and became the first white man to visit the site of present-day Toronto. (ILLUSTRATION BY C.W. JEFFERYS)*

THE LIFE AND TIMES OF
 # ÉTIENNE BRÛLÉ

Champlain's protégé and the first
coureur de bois, Brûlé's achievements were
overshadowed by an act of treachery.

UNWITTINGLY, HE WAS THE role model for generations to come in New France. Etienne Brûlé was the first coureur de bois, an inspiration to the bold, the restless, and those who despised the settled life. He represented the carefree life of the Indian brave, moving silently through the forests as the spirit moved him. The bane of clergy, governors and merchants, Brûlé and the coureurs de bois would range the continent, going where no white man had gone before.

He was born of French peasant stock and came to New France as Champlain's servant in 1608. Two years later, drawn by the great rivers to the north, he asked to be allowed to live among the Indians. Champlain, eager to train interpreters, entrusted him to the Algonquin chief Iroquet for a year. Taking up a paddle, the 18-year-old Brûlé journeyed up the Ottawa, then moved on to Huronia before rendezvousing with Champlain at the Lachine Rapids in June 1611. The former servant had been transformed. Tanned, lean and hard, dressed in buckskins and fluent in the Algonquin and Huron dialects, he would spend the rest of his life living as an Indian, opening up the fur trade and acting as Champlain's agent until that fateful day in 1629.

In the summer of 1615, Champlain once again met Brûlé at the Lachine Rapids, this time to plan an attack on the Iroquois. The Iroquois had been the mortal enemies of the French since the day Champlain had fired his arquebus at their chiefs on the shores of the lake that now bears his name. Now, the Iroquois were pressing Champlain's allies in Huronia and interfering with the flow of furs to the little settlement at Quebec — trading being its sole means of support.

On July 9, they started up the Ottawa, crossed Lake Nipissing, and then descended the French River into Lake Huron. Turning their canoes south, they landed about seven kilometres away from present-day Penetanguishene on August 1. Throughout the summer, they traveled from village to village in Huronia, exhorting the chiefs to take up the attack against the Iroquois. In mid-August, at Cahaiagué, a council of war came together, and 500 Huron were soon on their way into Iroquois country. Brûlé was dispatched to enlist the aid of the Susquehanna, a powerful tribe that inhabited lands south of Lake Erie.

The main party moved by canoe past Orillia and Peterborough, down the Trent River and into the Bay of Quinte, then across Lake Ontario. They entered Iroquois country somewhere near Stony Point, N.Y., and headed inland on foot toward an Onondaga fort, near what is now Syracuse. Only a siege would do as the fort was protected by a lake and streams and walled with palisades topped by fighting galleries. Champlain set the Hurons to work with hatchets and knives to build mantelets (bulletproof screens for gunners) and a cavalier (a movable tower from which they could fire down on the defenders). On October 11, under a rain of stones and arrows, they carried it forward. Three Frenchmen opened fire from the top compelling the Onondaga to abandon the galleries and fight from cover. The attack faltered, Champlain finding himself in charge of men "who do what they like" and who shouted so much so that "one could not make oneself heard." Wounded in the leg, he was carried to the rear on an Indian's back.

The French and Hurons camped outside the walls for a week, then abandoned the siege on October 18, two days before Brûlé arrived with the Susquehanna. After wintering in Huronia, Champlain returned to Quebec. To the inhabitants, he seemed like a man back from the dead.

Brûlé's failure to bring support to Champlain and the Hurons in time was not due to any fault of his own. He made a quick descent to Lake Orillia and down the Humber River, thus becoming the first white man to visit the site of the city of Toronto. Crossing Lake Ontario, he skirted Iroquois country, reaching safety in the upper waters of the Susquehanna River. The Susquehanna chiefs were friendly, but inclined to be dilatory. Days were wasted in useless powwows and council meetings. By the time a war party was gathered and on its way, it was too late. When he failed to return to Quebec, Champlain was convinced that his one-time servant was dead. No one could have been more alive and active.

After the failure of the expedition against the Iroquois, he began the travels that would have made him famous had a final act of treachery not sullied his reputation. He paddled down the Susquehanna and reached the northern tip of Chesapeake Bay. On the way back, the Iroquois captured him. Good fortune and a ruse helped him escape torture and death. When one of his captors snatched a religious medal he wore around his neck, the skies suddenly darkened, and thunder and lightning rent the air. Brûlé declared that the storm was a sign of divine intervention and persuaded the fearful Iroquois to release him.

He had been the first to ascend the Ottawa and the Mattawa, following its course to Lake Nipissing and the French River, thus establishing the route to the Huron country. He had also been the first to set eyes on Lake Huron, Lake Erie, and Lake Ontario. Returning to Huron country, he set out with a war party past Michilimackinac and into the waters of Lake Superior, the *Grand Lac*. It is also likely that he journeyed into Lake Michigan. If so, he was the first white man to glimpse all of the Great Lakes.

Brûlé left no records, no journals, and no letters. He is occasionally glimpsed in the writings of Champlain and of the Jesuit fathers who felt that his licentiousness mocked their teachings. He flits through their writings like a wraith through the forest: mysterious and almost invisible. No clear description of him exists, but it is known that he always dressed as an

Étienne Brûlé was captured by the Iroquois on his return from Chesapeake Bay. He tricked them into releasing him by claiming to have brought on a thunderstorm.

Indian and that he was enormously strong. He probably married in the Indian fashion of the time, taking wives and putting them aside as fancy dictated. Father Gabriel Sagard, who had been his friend, acknowledged sadly that he was "much addicted to women." It is probable, too, that he became active in the fur trade.

The fur trade was the monopoly of the French monarch and his recognized agents, or farmers as they came to be known. They were responsible for the export of all the "peltry" of Canada. Beaver and fox would adorn the upper classes in Europe, while the skins of the less valuable deer, muskrat and moose would be made into work clothes for the lower orders. No one else was allowed to participate in the trade, except of course the Indians who shot, trapped and cured the pelts. Because of this monopoly, the farmers could fix the price they paid the Indians — usually in trading trinkets or tools — as low as possible while collecting a handsome commission.

As word of Brûlé's adventures filtered back to Quebec, a new type of Canadian began to interfere with the monopoly. He was the coureur de bois, eager to live the supposedly carefree life of the Indian brave, and also to trade with him. Some left wives and families behind, providing for them as best they could. Others completely abandoned white civilization and, like Brûlé, adopted the customs and ways of the Indians. To the chagrin of the farmers, they would often sell their furs at a much higher price to English and Dutch merchants to the south. Boston and Albany flourished while the towns of New France sank into poverty, largely due to the defection of young men needed to till the soil. By Frontenac's time, orders had been issued to suppress the coureurs de bois. Anyone who ventured out into the forests without the King's permission faced the death penalty. Few were deterred.

The enormous profits to be made in the fur trade attracted the piratical Kirkes to Quebec. Shareholders in the London-based Company of Merchant Adventurers, they wrested the colony away from the French in 1629, bundling Champlain and 16 starving companions aboard their ships as prisoners of war. Champlain knew that Frenchmen had led the Kirkes up the St. Lawrence. At Tadoussac, he would learn their identities.

Weary and dejected, he was allowed to go ashore before sailing into exile. As he walked along a wharf, two men were pointed out to him as having belonged to the party of four who acted as guides to the enemy. With rising indignation, he approached the pair, who hung back and seemed anxious to get away. To his astonishment and sorrow, he recognized one of them as Etienne Brûlé. He proceeded to berate him at great length. A version of what he said is recorded in the Jesuit *Relations*, but it has unquestionably been rephrased, for it is a stilted harangue, hardly reflecting the heat of the moment. It is said that Brûlé, holding his head down and shuffling in embarrassment, made no defence except to say that he knew the French garrison had no hope of resisting successfully, and so it had not seemed to him wrong to act with the English.

Brûlé went back to Huron country, his days of glory and achievement at an end. He settled down in the village of Toanché, on Penetanguishene Bay, a place of great natural beauty. He no longer traveled, and sank into a life of sloth and degradation, frequently quarreling with his neighbours. Three years later, the Hurons murdered him, cut up his body, and ate it. He was 41 years old. No one knows their reason, but they may have resented his betrayal of their friend Champlain. They would not be punished as Champlain assured them of this on his return to Canada in 1633. Brûlé, he said, was no longer considered a Frenchman.

✑ LA BELLE HÉLÈNE

Champlain takes a bride, the 12-year-old
daughter of a wealthy Huguenot family.

THERE HAD BEEN LITTLE TIME for romance in Champlain's life. In 1610, however, after his first victory against the Iroquois, he returned to France and took a wife. The bride was a child of 12.

Champlain was 43 years old and at the peak of his fame and career when he exchanged wedding vows in the Church of St. Germain l'Auxerrois with Hélène Bouillé, the daughter of a wealthy Huguenot and secretary to King Louis XIII. Because of her age, the marriage contract stipulated that she must remain with her parents for at least two years before joining her husband in Canada.

She was a beautiful, mature and spirited woman of 22 when she finally sailed for Quebec with four servants and as many trunks packed with the latest Parisian finery. Daintiness was all the fashion, with wrist cuffs of point lace, slashed sleeves, and trim polonian shoes. As she stepped ashore onto a dilapidated wharf, her new home must have astonished her.

RIGHT: With the Habitation near ruin, Champlain set artisans to work to repair it. (ILLUSTRATION BY C.W. JEFFERYS)

OPPPOSITE PAGE: In 1620, when Hélène Bouillé was 22, she joined Champlain at Quebec City. The daughter of the King's secretary and used to a life of luxury, she returned to France four years later and later became a nun of the Ursuline Order. (PAINTING BY FRANK CRAIG, PUBLIC ARCHIVES OF CANADA)

Merchants, black-robed Jesuit priests and Ursuline nuns hurried about their business as chickens and pigs wandered the muddy streets of the little settlement. Indians in buckskins, traders and unwashed coureurs de bois, just back from *le pays d'en haut,* haggled over bales of fur. Recently, Indians camping near Quebec had killed two Frenchmen in a drunken quarrel, and relations were tense. Ferociously painted and haughty Iroquois braves were visiting the settlement to discuss a peace treaty between the Five Nations and the French. The inhabitants, raised on tales of their cruelty, watched them with anxious eyes. Suspicion grew that they had come to spy out the land, and Champlain hastily took steps to improve the settlement's defences.

Above the town, Fort Saint-Louis was under construction behind a ravelin and moat, near Louis Hébert's kitchen garden, and was soon firing cannon at dawn and dusk to give warning that a vigilant watch was being kept. The Jesuits and Récollets were building in the valley of the St. Charles River – Récollets on the right bank, Jesuits on the left. Nearby, Hébert, with the help of a servant, had started another garden, growing corn, peas and beans. Less than eight hectares of land had been cleared, not enough to grow crops for the entire settlement. Game, abundant in the encircling forests, was a staple in the settlers' diet.

The Habitation was a near ruin. Sinking into its foundations, the walls sagged, the floors were uneven and the doors and windows fit so badly that it was full of drafts and could not be properly heated in winter. It reeked of mildew, as the roof leaked and water ran down the walls. The first winter was a time of difficult adjustment for the delicately raised young woman from Paris, and there was very little for her to do. Champlain, no doubt, did what he could to ease the strain, setting artisans to work to repair the house and ensuring the larders were full to ward off scurvy. It is not on record that he started anything like the *Ordre de Bons Temps* of his Port Royal days, to add spice to the long, dull winter nights. It was a relieved man who wrote in his journal on May 6 that "the cherry trees have begun to open their buds and the hepaticas are springing from the soil."

Very little is known about his marriage. He avoided the subject in the journals he maintained so faithfully, setting down the date of her arrival and the date she left, nothing more. He named Île Sainte Hélène, just off the island of Montreal, in her honour. A convert to Catholicism, she became deeply religious and was noted for her kindness. The Indians were drawn to her, as were the clergy of the colony. She was said to have frequently worn a gold chain, with a small mirror, around her neck, and the Indians counted it a great privilege to look at it and see themselves reflected there, believing this meant that she always kept them in her heart. She instructed their children in the catechism. But she was a very unhappy young woman, and returned to France in 1624. Ten years after Champlain's death, she became an Ursuline nun, taking the name Sister Hélène d'Augustin, and founded a convent at Meaux where she died on December 20, 1654.

There had been no children born of the marriage. Four years after Hélène's departure, Champlain adopted three Indian girls, aged 11, 12, and 15, presented to him in gratitude for feeding a starving band. He named them Faith, Hope, and Charity, and raised them as his daughters. Faith soon returned to her people, but Hope and Charity remained with him until he was taken captive by the Kirkes in 1629. He begged in vain to be allowed to take the girls with him. He made provisions for their care, but when he returned to Quebec in 1633, they had reverted to native life and disappeared into the forests.

The father of Canada was not to know even the satisfaction of an adopted family.

OPPOSITE PAGE: *This English musketeer, armed with an arquebus, would have been stationed at Port Royal and Quebec between 1629 and 1632. (RICHARD CATON – WOODVILLE, BROWN UNIVERSITY)*

WESTWARD HO! THE BRITISH ARRIVE

The English arrive in North America amid territorial wars with Spain, Holland, and France. Regulars, Rangers, and citizen militia are established in the American colonies.

ONE OF THE MORE popular parlour paintings in English drawing rooms was a depiction of an Elizabethan "old salt" describing to a wide-eyed boy his adventures in the New World.

While the English were perhaps a little behind the French in their settlement of North America, they certainly arrived in increasing numbers until they eventually outnumbered France's adventurers.

In Europe, conflict was frequent and, despite a series of shifting alliances, the two nations found themselves on opposite sides in most of the wars. At the same time, English and French newcomers to the New World – allied to native Indian tribes – lived in an almost constant state of hostilities, or, at best, fearful apprehension of raids, skirmishes and various levels of conflict.

Fleet of galleons from the Spanish Basque lands, anchored off Labrador around 1560. The Basques maintained a lucrative fishery here for more than a century. (PAINTING BY RICHARD SCHLECHT, *national geographic society*)

At first the English aggression was carried out at sea. Off Newfoundland especially, English pirates and privateers, jealous of intrusion by Spanish, French, and Portuguese invasions of 'their' lucrative fishing grounds, would often destroy foreign fishing settlements and vessels, frequently seizing the catch as spoils of an undeclared war.

During the 16th century, England had revolutionized sea warfare by removing the cumbersome "castles" at the bow and sterns of naval vessels, which were crammed with armed seamen who would grapple, board and hopefully capture their foes. In their place they installed broadsides of muzzle-loading cannon, with which they would stand off and pound their enemies into submission. (In later years, this innovation was used to good effect by the Sieur d'Iberville, who routed a superior-sized English fleet in Hudson Bay. The imitators had learned well.)

Occasionally, English sea captains were licensed by the Sovereign to harry and seize booty from actual or potential enemies. One family, the notorious Kirke brothers, harassed French shipping in the St. Lawrence estuary and, in 1629, forced the surrender of the settlement of Quebec. Ironically, the Kirkes were French by birth.

Meanwhile, wars of varying duration and severity raged throughout Europe. Usually, the conflicts in North America, although concurrent, had little part in the overall strategic picture. Any significant activity in the Western Hemisphere tended to centre on the spice and sugar-rich islands of the Caribbean, many of which changed flags several times.

In North America, survival was the first priority. Early conflicts were against native peoples, who naturally resented the Europeans taking over their hunt-

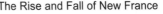

In December 1636, the colony of Massachusetts decreed that militia regiments should be formed. All adult males with the exception of clergy, doctors, and Harvard students were required to undergo a week's military training.
(RECONSTITUTION BY DON TROIANI, U.S. NATIONAL GUARD)

ing grounds. The first traders, and later settlers, were too busy seeking profits in the fur trade or, later, cultivating the virgin land. As time went on, skirmishes resulted from trade rivalry as Dutch, French and English traders protected their "turf." The noted historical writer, Thomas Costain, contrasted the philosophy and lifestyles of the English and French colonists. While Louis's subjects were strictly controlled by the Royal Governor, and would (usually) uphold his decrees, the English were more free spirited. Instead of one religion the different colonies covered a wide range of beliefs – from Massachusetts' Puritans through Pennsylvania's Quakers to Maryland's Catholics. Rather than one unified overseas department, the English colonies were all independent, chartered by the King, but often supported by groups of London speculators. The "divine right kings" – the keystone of French civil obedience – had gone by the board when Charles I was executed in Whitehall.

In 1613, the English (who had hitherto more or less remained south of what is now the Canada/U.S. border) showed signs of aggression and destroyed French settlements in Acadia. Britain later took possession of most of Acadia, which they renamed "Nova Scotia" (present-day Maritime Provinces and northern Maine).

During the 17th century, Britain engaged in three wars against the Dutch. As a result of these conflicts – fought here almost exclusively by colonial militias – the English gained New York and New Jersey. As happened time and again in North America, what was won by force of arms was lost by diplomacy: in the final war, Dutch naval and land forces recaptured New York, Albany, Long Island and New Jersey, only to cede them to the English under the final Treaty of Westminster. One significant outcome was that the Iroquois, previously allied with the Dutch, now sided with the English – a situation which had serious and far-reaching effects on French Canada. For once (in the Third Dutch War), Britain and France were allied against Holland in Europe. Ironically, during the same period, the English (sometimes abetted by Dutch settlers) continued their forays against French settlements.

On land, apart from clashes between rival groups of fur traders, the English appeared more interested in fighting each other than in waging war against France. One notable exception was a foray in 1669 by William Phips, who fitted out a fleet at his own expense, and, with a band of New England volunteers, raided Acadia and seized Port Royal. (France retook it, but in vain as the Treaty of Ryswick restored it to England seven years later.) An attempt to seize Quebec City the following year was thwarted by the weather, terrain, and a smallpox epidemic among the English. (The church of Notre-Dame-des-Victoires in Quebec's lower town commemorates the "victory.")

Eventually the New England colonies decided that "unity is strength," and Massachusetts joined four other colonies in the New England Confederation. Among other advantages, this provided a unified military command. Its main claim to fame was in King Philip's War where, following raids by the Wampanaog Aboriginals under "King" Philip, the Confederation conducted a successful campaign in the Connecticut Valley region.

With the exception of France, who had provided two regiments of regular troops, as well as the Compagnies Franches de la Marine who were officered by local minor nobility, few regulars came into the picture until the end of the War of the Spanish Succession (which gave Newfoundland, Acadia and Hudson's Bay to Britain). Following the 1713 Treaty of Utrecht, six battalions of Duke of Marlborough's veterans were sent to protect the English settlers. (This was not a wholly generous gesture on the part of Queen Anne, as the colonists were expected to raise the taxes to pay the occupation force – an imposition that played a major part in the American Revolution.)

During the first half of the 18th century, minor clashes continued. (This resulted in a new addition to the military dictionary as the term *petite guerre*, translated to the Spanish *guerrilla*, was used to describe the unconventional tactics.) Although often conducted concurrently with the major European battles, they really had little to do with the *casus belli*. Europe's wars were waged over religious and political issues or in revenge for real or imagined insults. (In 1739, Britain went to war with Spain over an allegation that Spanish officials had cut off a Welsh sea captain's ear).

Later, in King George's War (1740-1748) both sides, aided by Indian allies, invaded each other's settlements. Louisbourg was captured by a joint operation of colonial troops and royal naval vessels, only to be restored (again) to the French at the Treaty of Aix-la-Chapelle.

Lacking financial and material support from their homeland, the colonies had been forced to organize militia forces. The first unit formed, in 1638, was Boston's Ancient and Honorable Artillery Company (which still exists). The colony of Massachusetts instituted a draft requiring all males (with a few exceptions such as clergy, doctors and Harvard students) to undergo a week's military training. As each colony's militia was under the governor's rule, the command and control structure was often lacking, as the independent New Englanders were reluctant to soldier under any other colony's control. The citizen soldier was provided with a musket, but often his "uniform" consisted of his own clothing with a sprig of leaves or scrap of cloth in his tricorne hat.

What he did have, and what his better-equipped English Army reinforcements lacked, was an awareness of Indian tactics and the art of living in and using the forests. The "Lobsterbacks" (so called not only because of their scarlet tunics but also because of the prevalence of flogging as a means of maintaining discipline) were at a disadvantage. Not only were their heavy serge uniforms, leather neck-stocks, pipeclayed gaiters and tall "grenadier" hats unsuitable for wilderness expeditions, their tactics – which had served them so well at Blenheim and Ramillies – proved ineffective in North America's forests, especially against natives who knew nothing of conventional warfare.

Some commanders had insight. The cumbersome, slow loading matchlock muskets were replaced by the flintlocks (an innovation that was subsequently adopted in Europe). Heavy armour had also been abandoned except in the case of some cavalry regiments. The horsemen jealously guarded their claim as the senior branch, although they were not very effective once they had left the roads and cleared fields of the settled areas for the forest wilderness.

Later, in time for the Seven Years War (also known as the French and Indian War in North America), improvements were made. Each infantry battalion included two flank companies, a Grenadier company and a light infantry company. The former's role was to launch the assault, using (naturally) hand grenades. The light infantry company, although at first consisting of the "hard bargains," was later used for scouting, skirmishing and screening the main body (which continued to march along the forest trails in vulnerable columns). Eventually, they became an elite component – moving quickly in response to bugle calls, unburdened by the several kilograms of equipment their unfortunate line company comrades had to carry. In time, the light infantry company became one of the more resourceful and independent sub-units of the regiment.

In addition to the royal troops arriving from Europe and the West Indies, regular regiments were raised in North America.

These combined the training and discipline of the English Army with the wilderness know-how of the colonists. (The colonial militia was not always as dependable as one might wish, for at times they left the expeditionary forces to return home in light of real or imaginary slights.) Perhaps the most notable American units were the Rangers or rifle regiments. Recruited in part from German settlers in Pennsylvania, and adopting the accurate frontier rifle, these elite units would penetrate the forests and frequently beat hostile Indians at their own game. Not for them were the scarlet and pipeclay; instead, dark green uniforms or buckskins were the order of dress. (One Canadian regiment, the Queen's York Rangers, claims an unbroken succession from one of these units, Rogers' Rangers, of Northwest Passage fame.)

More of the King's troops arrived in North America or were recruited locally. Eventually, as frequently happens in the guerrilla war continuum, the minor skirmishes gave place to set-piece battles, and the Seven Years War had begun. Braddock, Montcalm, Wolfe, and even a young George Washington entered the scene.

OPPOSITE PAGE: *In the absence of her husband, Marie-Jacquelin de La Tour commanded the garrison of Fort La Tour in 1645. (NEW BRUNSWICK MUSEUM)*

✍ MADAME DE LA TOUR'S LAST STAND

Raised in a convent in France, Marie-Jacquelin dreamed of high adventure and battles in far-away lands where women too led armies.

NO PLACE IN CANADA has been more fought over. Founded by the French in 1604, Port Royal in Nova Scotia's Annapolis Basin, Champlain's "*si beau et bon pays*," has been settled and abandoned, revived, sacked, returned to France by treaty and then reconquered by the English. It was also the setting for one of the deadliest feuds in Canadian history – a feud that led to a six-year civil war.

In 1636, four years after France regained the colony under the terms of the Treaty of Saint-Germain-en-Laye, Charles de Menou d'Aulnay, a 32-year-old aristocratic former naval officer, stepped ashore with 40 families and 12 Capuchin friars determined to rule not only Port Royal but all of Acadia and to crush anyone who stood in his way. Within a few months he had built a manor house, a mill and a fort garrisoned by 300 soldiers with

60 cannons. Ruling like a feudal lord, he granted land to the settlers, courted the Micmacs and muscled his way into the local fur trade.

The historic enemies of the French in Acadia were the English colonists to the south. But d'Aulnay's greatest enemy was closer to home: Charles de Saint-Etienne de La Tour of Fort Sainte-Marie, across the Bay of Fundy (at present-day Saint John, NB).

An ambitious Norman, de La Tour had spent most of his life in Acadia. When Port Royal was laid to waste by Samuel Argall and his Virginia free-booters in 1613, he took to the woods with Jean de Biencourt, the colony's leader, and a small group of survivors. Subsisting on fish and game and living like Indians, they finally succeeded in building a new fort at Cape Sable, which they named Fort Loméron. In time, de La Tour prospered in the fur trade and laid claim to Acadia as Biencourt's designated successor. The French court, however, disallowed his claim, suspecting him of double-dealing with the English. Enraged, he refused to acknowledge the upstart d'Aulnay's authority.

De La Tour's staunchest ally was his young bride, the fiery Marie-Jacquelin, daughter of a Le Mans barber whom he had married by proxy. Educated in a convent at Nogent-le-Rotou, as a girl she had poured over popular romances like "Amadis of Gaul" with its themes of high adventure, patrician heroes and heroines, and battles in far-away lands where women too led armies. Joining her husband at Fort Sainte-Marie, she encouraged him to take the offensive against d'Aulnay. The impetuous de La Tour needed little encouragement.

Sailing for the Annapolis Basin, de La Tour and his wife were confronted by two of d'Aulnay's pinnaces, the *Notre Dame* and the *Saint-François*. D'Aulnay would later claim that de La Tour fired the first shot "without cause." Whoever started it, the duel was savage, but short. At first, the fortune of war was with the de La Tours whose ship's cannon loosed a crippling broadside that brought down the *Notre Dame*'s mainmast and mortally wounded several men. But the advantage soon slipped to d'Aulnay, a trained naval officer fighting in his home harbour. Driving them into the shallows among the islands and hammering them with chain-shot, he forced the de La Tours to strike their colours and surrender.

The master of Port Royal asserted self-righteously in the imperious third person that de La Tour "and his mistress" were "most humanely treated by the Sieur d'Aulnay who could at one blow have avenged himself on him for all past injuries." After a brief imprisonment, they were allowed to return to Fort Sainte-Marie, Marie-Jacquelin determined never to fall into his hands again.

After the quarrel had been referred to the King, de La Tour was stripped of his commission and ordered to return to France. D'Aulnay sailed to Fort Sainte-Marie personally to deliver the royal edict. Rather than obey, a contemporary document relates that de La Tour "snatched the papers, crushed them between his hands, abused the envoys roundly, put them into prison and held them for above a year." D'Aulnay could do little more than blockade the fort in the hopes of starving the garrison into submission.

Slipping through the blockade in the dead of night, the de La Tours turned to Boston for help. Appearing before the town's magistrates, they convinced them that d'Aulnay was an usurper holding them hostage in their own fort. They were allowed to hire four ships – the 100-ton *Seabridge*, the *Increase*, the *Philip and Mary*, and the little *Greyhound* – with 200 seamen and 38 guns, using their holdings in Acadia as security. At the sight of the de La Tours' newly-acquired fleet, d'Aulnay immediately cut his hawsers, lifted the blockade and fled back to Port Royal.

The following spring, Marie-Jacquelin sailed to France to drum up support for her husband. Much to her dismay, the court had had quite enough of their antics and placed her under house arrest. Faced with the death penalty, she escaped to England. Boarding a ship bound for Boston, she made her way back to Fort Sainte-Marie just as d'Aulnay was delivering yet another order from His Majesty. Once again, he was met with curses and insults. Madame de La Tour now counseled her husband to renounce his faith and become a Protestant. This, she reasoned, would appeal to the religious fervor of the New Englanders and, coupled with an offer of a share in the spoils, would lead to their enthusiastic help in wresting Acadia from d'Aulnay. In April 1645, de La Tour left Marie-Jacquelin in charge and set off for Boston.

This was just the moment that d'Aulnay had been waiting for. After calling up every man in Port Royal capable of carrying a musket, he set sail for Fort Sainte-Marie aboard the 16-gun *Grand Cardinal* and a fleet of smaller

The de La Tours would have sailed warships similar to these, common in the 1630s. (NAC/ c109028)

ships. Well-schooled in siegecraft, he tacked into the Saint John River to within pistol-range of the fort, and landed a shore party to set up a battery close to the walls. When Madame de La Tour refused to capitulate, spurning his offer with "insults and blasphemies," he opened fire.

Broadsides raked the fort. The river basin echoed the crack and roar of cannon. Solid shot howled overhead and salvoes of grapeshot rattled on tiled roofs and shattered windows. Fires in the storehouse and living quarters of the fort were barely kept in check by buckets of water carried from the well. Musketry crackled from the parapets as powder-blackened cannoneers on both sides swabbed gun barrels, weighed, loaded, and fired again and again. Those who served the guns of Fort Sainte-Marie had to make every shot count, for while d'Aulnay's powder supply seemed inexhaustible, theirs was running low.

Madame de La Tour, La Commandante, directed the defence of the fort, proving herself a brave, capable and determined warrior. For four days and nights, clad in a steel breastplate, oblivious to the crash of shot, the sulphurous stink of gunpowder, smoke from burning timbers and the smell of blood and sweat, she strode the walls sighting guns and encouraging the men. Jagged pieces of wood lay in heaps, roof tiles and broken glass littered the flagstones, and part of the palisade collapsed into the defensive ditch. As d'Aulnay and his men launched a full-scale assault over the shattered walls, she snatched up a pike and led a counterattack, yielding only under condition that d'Aulnay gave quarter to all. But that was not to be. In the shambles of the fort, with a rope around her neck, "as though she had been the greatest villain," she was forced to watch as d'Aulnay hanged her remaining men "to serve as a memorial and example to posterity of so obstinate a rebellion." Heartbroken, she died in captivity three weeks later. Her infant son was then sent to France.

D'Aulnay returned to Port Royal the undisputed master of Acadia. However, his triumph was short-lived. He died of exposure in May 1650, after his canoe capsized near the mouth of the Annapolis River. Legend has it that he was towed ashore with his head held underwater by an Indian he had beaten three days earlier. He is buried beneath the steps of the church of Port Royal in accordance with his testament, "entreating all who pass by to have pity for a person who merits only the thunderbolts and chastisement of a justly angry God."

De La Tour was forced to rely on the charity of friends in Boston before moving on to Quebec. Learning of his rival's death, he hurried to France to present his case at court. In February 1651, at the age of 60, this indomitable survivor was commanded by the Queen Regent to maintain and conserve Acadia as "he would have continued to do so if he had not been prevented by the now dead Charles de Menou d'Aulnay." Returning to Acadia as governor and lieutenant general, he married d'Aulnay's widow who bore him five children. Marie-Jacquelin would have relished the irony.

A 17th century French print depicts the weapons and equipment employed in Madame de La Tour's bitter battle for Fort Sainte Marie.

⇗ THE JESUIT *RELATIONS*

Published annually in Paris for 40 years, the Jesuit Relations *introduced the Old World to the New.*

FOUNDED IN PARIS IN 1534 by St. Ignatius Loyola and St. Francis Xavier, the Society of Jesus, or Jesuits, would play a prominent role in the development of New France.

Three remarkable men formed the Jesuit advance guard: Gabriel Lalemant, Jean de Brébeuf, and Enemond Masse. Disciplined, courageous and burning with the religious zeal of the Counter-Reformation, they arrived in Quebec without fanfare. Taking up temporary quarters with the Récollets on the St. Charles River, they set to work familiarizing themselves with native languages before building a simple but stout house behind a palisade of tall timbers. Perhaps eager for the martyrdom that beckoned, they set forth into the forests as soon as their base had been established. Lalemant and Brébeuf went to live among the Hurons and were soon writing to the General of the Society "...we have baptized more than ninety."

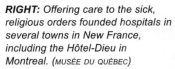

RIGHT: *Offering care to the sick, religious orders founded hospitals in several towns in New France, including the Hôtel-Dieu in Montreal.* (MUSÉE DU QUÉBEC)

OPPOSITE PAGE: *The Jesuits established missions throughout Huronia and began their efforts in converting the Hurons to Christianity.*

Interest in Canada had been sparked by Champlain's several volumes and by the Récollet missionary Gabriel Sagard's "Le Grand Voyage au Pays des Hurons." But the Jesuits' annual report, *Relations*, would become a publishing phenomenon stimulating their efforts to convert the Indians and encourage immigration. The *Relations* of 1636 noted: "Why cannot the great forests of New France largely furnish the ships for the Old? Who doubts that there are mines of iron, copper, and other metals? ...All those who work in wood and iron will find employment here."

Relations' main purpose was to gain support for missionary work. Readers donated toward the establishment of a mission near Quebec, which soon grew to include a hospital, chapel, and school. Donations also supported missions at Sillery and Trois-Rivières as well as those in Huronia. And it was an avid reader of *Relations*, Jérôme Le Royer de La Dauversière, who formed a society to colonize the Island of Montreal.

The most regular correspondent was Father Paul le Jeune who became the Superior at Quebec. He had the capacity to convey in what he wrote the fervour of the priests in the missions. His letters, filled with stories of their trials and triumphs, and of the long and ferocious Indian wars, began to attract much attention in France. Taken up by the most prominent printer in Paris and published in vellum-bound volumes, they were put on the market at twenty sols. Sales were enormous and publication was kept up for over 40 years.

To his great astonishment, Father le Jeune discovered that he had become famous. Diplomats and soldiers, priests, nuns and working people were reading his letters and offering their assistance. So much so that he wrote: "The Ursuline mothers write me with such ardor that if the door were open a city of nuns would be formed and there would be found ten sisters to one pupil." He soon became aware of the mixed quality of the settlers the letters were attracting. "Every year the ships bring us many people," he said. "This number like coin is of mingled gold and base alloy; it is composed of choice and well-selected souls, and of others indeed base and degraded."

The success of *Relations* stimulated the missionaries to further efforts. More priests were sent out to join the fathers in the field. Sometimes, soldiers and workmen went with them. An example of the collaboration that developed was the voyage into Huron country of highly skilled artisans to build the chapel at Sainte-Marie. Master carpenters and joiners travelled by canoe, carrying their tools and much of the building material with them.

Over the years, the Jesuits began to discuss matters of a lighter nature in the *Relations,* perhaps sensing that readers would be repelled by the repetition of horrors in their accounts of the Indian wars. The habits and beliefs, customs, likes and dislikes of the various tribes are described. Father Ragueneau, among others, informs us that the Hurons disliked the white skins of the French and found curly hair and beards loathsome. It was not uncommon, he tells us, for a Huron to look into a bearded Frenchman's face, shudder, and say, "Ugh, how ugly you are!"

The *Relations* of the 1640s are much darker. They tell of Iroquois attacks, the destruction of Huronia and the martyrdom of the Jesuit missionaries. Dark they may be, but they became – and remain – the finest primary source of this period in Canadian history.

LEFT: *The main purpose of the Jesuit* Relations *was to gain support for missionary work by detailing their trials and triumphs in New France. This* Relations *cover is for the year 1634.*

OPPOSITE PAGE: *Jesuit Father Gabriel Lalemant joined Jean de Brébeuf in Huronia just six months before being martyred on March 17, 1649 by the Iroquois. Sainthood was conferred upon both in 1930.* (PAC/NMC-1664)

❧ THE RUIN OF HURONIA

French missions and the proud Huron nation were destroyed by the Iroquois in the 1640s.

AFTER EIGHT HUNDRED MILES of paddling and portage, travellers from Quebec came into a little river that runs into Georgian Bay near the present-day site of Midland, Ontario. They then steered their canoes into a man-made channel that ran from the river to a gate in a palisade of logs. Inside was the mission of Sainte-Marie, an island of French civilization in the heart of Huronia.

Etienne Brûlé had led the way into Huron country on his first great voyage in 1611. Champlain wintered there four years later and then came scores of missionaries, traders, and coureurs de bois. It was an arduous journey as one of Brûlé's friends, Récollet Gabriel Sagard, recounts: "...one must make up one's mind to endure and suffer more than could be imagined, from hunger, from sleeping always on the bare ground in the open country, from walking with great labour in water and bogs, and in some

These Huron chiefs escaped from the Iroquois massacres of 1648-1649, eventually settling near Quebec City. (METROPOLITAN TORONTO LIBRARY)

places over rocks, and through dark, thick woods, from rain on one's back and all the evils that the season and weather can inflict, and from being bitten by a countless swarm of mosquitoes and midges."

The outer palisade of the mission sheltered a hospital, workshops, a granary, and chapel. There were also longhouses, kitchens, carpenter and blacksmith shops, all surrounded by a series of walls and bastions of considerable strength. By March 1649, there were 58 Europeans at Sainte-Marie, including 18 Jesuit priests, farmers, fur traders, and 22 soldiers. Homesick Frenchmen loved the reassurance of a life regulated by the ringing of bells and by the seasons and festivals of the Church. To the Hurons, Sainte-Marie was a sanctuary, a place to worship, to be tended in illness and buried in death.

Allies of the French since the earliest days of settlement, the Huron homeland stretched from Lake Simcoe through Muskoka to the rolling, wooded and beautiful region around Georgian Bay. Numbering about twenty thousand, the Hurons lived in more than thirty villages. They hunted, fished, and tilled the land, burning off the trees and underbrush, and planting corn, beans, pumpkins and tobacco. The land was crowded, but it provided them with one great advantage: they were widely separated from their enemies of long standing, the fierce and predatory Iroquois.

Of all Indian tribes, the Hurons seemed to respond most readily to Christian teachings, and in each of the four tribal families into which they were

The Huron, Petun, Neutral and Iroquois nations built longhouse villages like this one, reconstructed at Delaware, Ontario. (CHARLES J. HUMBER COLLECTION)

divided – the Bear, the Rock, the Cord and the Deer – the number of converts rose steadily.

By the 1640s, the Jesuits had established 12 missions in Huronia. Eager to embrace any hardship, even martyrdom, to spread their faith, they found Indian life in the villages very different from the discipline, order, and comfort they enjoyed at Sainte-Marie.

The Hurons lived in longhouses shared by many families. Father Gabriel Lalemant, who would die at the hands of the Iroquois, recalled that "if you go to visit them in their cabins – and you must go there oftener than once a day, if you would perform your duty as you ought – you will find there a miniature picture of hell, seeing nothing ordinarily but fire and smoke and on every side naked bodies, black and half-roasted, mingled pell-mell with the dogs, which are held as dear as the children of the house, and share the beds, plates and food of their masters. Everything is in a cloud of dust and, if you go within, you will not reach the end of the cabin before you are completely covered with soot, filth and dirt." Undaunted, the Jesuits preached and increasingly tended the sick and dying. European diseases were now ravaging the Hurons and their numbers had decreased by half.

The conversion of the Hurons unintentionally reduced their effectiveness as allies of the French. No longer warriors, they asked for nothing more than to be left in peace to follow the injunctions of their spiritual fathers. Moreover, few of them had firearms which would lessen their chances of successfully defending themselves against their enemies. And through-out the existence of Sainte-Marie, the Hurons were continually under attack or threat of attack by the Hotinonsionni, as they called the five Iroquois nations – the Seneca, Onondaga, Cayuga, Oneida, and Mohawk.

Iroquois attacks were motivated by more than hatred for the Hurons. Well armed by the English and Dutch, they were anxious to control the fur trade and the Huron nation stood in the way. Hurons were frequently ambushed for their furs, then enslaved or tortured to death. Jesuits met the same fate. In 1642, Fathers René Goupil and Isaac Jogues were captured near Sorel on their way to Huronia and taken to Iroquois territory. Goupil was killed and Jogues tortured and mutilated before he was rescued by the Dutch. He would die a martyr four years later.

In 1645, the Hurons signed a tentative peace treaty with the Iroquois, but, within a year, they were on the warpath again, striking deeper and deeper into Huronia, laying entire villages to waste. Sainte-Marie was relatively secure behind its palisades, but the outlying missions were extremely vulnerable.

At Saint-Joseph, 30 kilometres west of what is now Orillia, Father Antoine Daniel had just finished early-morning mass in July 1647, when the Iroquois struck. At the first war cry, his panic-stricken parishioners crowded around him, pleading for protection. Realizing that this was the end for the village and his flock, he baptized those he could by sprinkling holy water from the font. Then, in his white alb and stole and carrying a large cross in front of him, he calmly walked to the door to face the Iroquois. He was cut down by hatchets, then shot. His body was consumed in the flames of his church.

Twelve hundred Iroquois spent the winter of 1648 on the frontiers of Huronia. In March 1649, they destroyed Saint-Ignace (near Waubaushene) then moved on to Saint-Louis. It, too, was overcome and set ablaze after a fierce fight against a band of eighty warriors led by Stephen Annaotaha, the bravest of Huron chiefs. It did not take long for the Iroquois to make a breach in the walls. They swarmed into the village, 1,000 strong, and the Hurons were soon killed or captured.

Among the captives were Fathers Jean de Brébeuf and Jérôme Lalemant who had stayed behind to care for the wounded and administer the last rites to the dying. They would die at the stake after suffering appalling

The Récollets was the first religious order to send priests to New France. They often served as teachers, missionaries, military chaplains, and parish priests.
(PUBLIC ARCHIVES OF CANADA)

tortures. Brébeuf, a large and powerful man, interested in all aspects of Huron life, had been much loved. Now, renegade Hurons among his tormenters "baptized" him with boiling water telling him that "you told us that the more one suffers on earth, the happier one is in heaven. We wish to make you happy; we do this because we love you and you ought to thank us for it." He died after four hours of agony. Lalemant was tortured throughout the night until an Iroquois, wearying of the sport, buried a hatchet in his skull.

On March 19, the Iroquois withdrew as swiftly as they had come. Prisoners who could not walk were tied to stakes in longhouses, which were then set on fire.

At Sainte-Marie, the Jesuits had seen the smoke rising from Saint-Louis and knew that their mission was doomed as the Iroquois had the advantages of surprise, numbers, and weapons. They knew too that they would come back and keep coming back until no one was left to oppose them. The Iroquois returned in force that summer, and terrified Hurons burned their crops and villages and fled into the forests. Some scattered into Petun, Neutral, and Erie territory. Others sought shelter within the walls of Sainte-Marie.

Realizing that they could not withstand a prolonged siege, the missionaries reluctantly evacuated Sainte-Marie and set off for Christian Island in Georgian Bay, along with the remaining Hurons. One Jesuit wrote: "That spot must be forsaken which I call our second fatherland, the cradle of this

Christian church, since it was the temple of God and the home of servants of Jesus Christ. For fear that our enemies, only too wicked, should profane the sacred place, and derive from it an advantage, we ourselves set fire to it, and beheld burn before our eyes, in less than an hour, our work of many years." They had laboured among the Hurons for 22 years and all that was left were trails through the forest and the blackened ruins of villages.

Between six and eight thousand fugitives crowded onto barren Christian Island. As winter set in, cholera and dysentery raged, and supplies ran low. By spring, only a few hundred Hurons were still alive, having been reduced to eating acorns and roots. They begged the Jesuits to take them to Quebec.

In the summer of 1650, 40 heavily armed Frenchmen set out from Montreal in a belated attempt to save Huronia. Along the Ottawa River, they met the remnants of the once proud Huron nation seeking refuge far from their ravaged homeland.

BELOW: *Abbé Hughes Pommier's painting,* The Jesuit Martyrs *(1665) combines the separate deaths of several early missionaries into one tale of horror. The deaths of Gabriel Lalemant and Jean de Brébeuf are shown in the right foreground.*

OPPOSITE PAGE: *With a pistol in each hand, Paul de Chomedey de Maisonneuve bravely stood his ground against a group of Iroquois. His authority and courage were no longer in question.* (DRAWING BY C.W. JEFFERYS)

❧ THE MUSTARD SEED

On January 6, 1643, Maisonneuve raises a cross on the mountain and a great city is born.

THE ISLAND OF MONTREAL cast a spell on all that saw it. Here, beneath the shadow of the mountain, two great rivers meet. The Ottawa, gathering volume from the tributaries that empty into it, comes down from the northern forests to mingle with the St. Lawrence, which flows in a northeasterly direction on its majestic way to the sea.

It was known as Hochelaga in Jacques Cartier's time, but when he climbed the mountain he named it Mont Royal. From its summit, he looked over "the finest land it is possible to see." Its beauty appealed to Champlain as well, although the village of Hochelaga had long since disappeared. The missionaries and traders who followed him saw it as one of the great natural crossroads of the continent they were so eager to explore. And in far-off Anjou it cast its spell on a penniless tax collector by the name of Jérôme Le Royer de La Dauversière.

A plump little man with a halting voice, de La Dauversière was a devoted reader of the Jesuit *Relations*. Slowly, a vision of the island began to form in his mind although there had been no description of it in anything written to date, nor had he spoken to anyone who had been there. The vision obsessed him so that he finally discussed it with his confessor, Father Chauveau, the rector of the Jesuit college at La Flèche. Chauveau was convinced that the vision had been granted him by God, and that he should devote the rest of his life to establishing a mission on the island.

In 1640, with the help of a sympathetic country abbé, he founded La Société de Notre-Dame de Montréal. Over the next 25 years, its wealthy members would contribute 600,000 livres (approximately three million dollars) to acquire a seigneury on the island and to outfit an expedition. Paul de Chomedy, Sieur de Maisonneuve, a 30-year-old soldier who had fought with distinction in the Dutch wars, was chosen to lead the expedition.

De La Dauversière spent the summer of 1640 scouring Anjou, Aunis and Normandy for suitable settlers, preferably unmarried men who would clear the land and defend the mission in exchange for wages, food, and lodging. One volunteer was a young woman, the beautiful Jeanne Mance, who arrived at La Rochelle on horseback, determined to sail with the expedition and open a hospital. A nurse by calling, an adventurer, and shrewd businesswoman, de La Dauversière could not deny her. By summer's end, he had recruited 60 souls.

The expedition put to sea in May 1641, aboard three ships. To their dismay, Maisonneuve and the settlers were received at Quebec with little enthusiasm. The Governor resented their autonomy and berated an undertaking that would put Frenchmen at the mercy of the hostile Iroquois. Maisonneuve insisted that he would go to Montreal "even if all the trees on that island were to change into so many Iroquois." And on Saturday, May 17, 1642, he stepped ashore on a spit of land now known as Pointe à Callières.

Later that day, mass was said at a simple altar adorned with cherry blossoms. "What you see is only a grain of mustard seed," the Jesuit Barthélemy Vimont said in a homily. "But this small seed will produce a tall tree that will bring forth wonders." Then tents were pitched, arms, implements, and provisions unloaded, and the first trees felled for a palisade.

More settlers arrived in August with much-needed provisions and word that the founding society had met in Notre-Dame de Paris to ask the Virgin to protect the settlement. On August 15, the Feast of the Assumption, they celebrated with pomp and cannon fire and formally named the settlement Ville-Marie.

Snow soon drifted over the little settlement and the inhabitants huddled in five small houses within its walls, living a communal life, finding "in Jesus Christ a single heart and a single soul." There was no sickness, something "never before remarked in new settlements," the Jesuit *Relations* recorded, attributing Ville-Marie's health to divine protection. But on Christmas Eve, the ice-jammed St. Lawrence flooded low-lying parts of the settlement. As the waters rose, Maisonneuve solemnly promised that if they were spared he would plant a cross on Mount Royal. When the waters subsided, he ordered a trail cut and a cross built and on January 6, 1643, carried it on his shoulders to the mountaintop. Three centuries later there would still be a cross on Mount Royal.

The settlers' arrival had not gone unnoticed by the Iroquois. Maisonneuve expected an attack at any time, and counted each day's delay a respite granted by a merciful God. That respite came to end in June 1643, when three men working outside the walls were killed and scalped. All that summer, Iroquois warriors harassed workers in the fields. Maisonneuve sent them out in groups under armed guard, the chapel bell signalling their departure and return. Some wanted to counterattack, but Maisonneuve refused, telling them they were "only a handful of people with little experience of the woods." A few scoffed that he was more pious than courageous.

To reassert his authority, Maisonneuve led a party of 30 men outside the walls to repel an attack on March 30, 1644. Forming up on a hill, which later became known as Place d'Armes, they fired volley after volley at the Iroquois who slipped elusively through the trees. Two settlers were killed and another wounded and, when their powder ran low, they broke and ran. Maisonneuve, a pistol in each hand, faced the enemy alone. An Iroquois chief lunged at him and he fired and missed. As they came to grips, Maisonneuve emptied his second pistol into his head. The Indians recovered the body and fled. Maisoneuve's courage was never questioned again.

Relations tells how the Iroquois, thirsting for revenge, "lay for entire days, each one behind a stump" or in tall grass so that "a man ten feet from his door was not in safety." Settlers carried muskets everywhere and cut gunports in the walls of their homes to protect themselves against enemies "behind a tree, under a pile of leaves or in a ditch, waiting for hours on end." Jeanne Mance's hospital was fortified with cannon while she tended the wounded – French and Indian alike.

Several settlers left, and by midsummer 1651, Ville-Marie's days seemed to be numbered. Maisonneuve knew that he must recruit more trained fighting men. When Jeanne Mance urged him to use a donation to her hospital to that end, he set sail for France on November 5, knowing too that the settlement was doomed if he failed. He would not return for two years.

At Quebec, the Governor believed that Ville-Marie would suffer the same fate as Sainte-Marie among the Hurons and the Huron nation. In the spring of 1653, he sent a ship up river with orders to the captain not to land unless he was certain that the settlement was still in French hands. Anchoring offshore in a dense fog, he could barely make out the palisade. He and his jittery crew beat a hasty retreat leaving the settlers "a little something to laugh about."

Somehow, Ville-Marie had survived and the settlers now had reason to laugh and rejoice. In June 1653, one of the five Iroquois nations, the Onondaga, made peace, finding the war much too costly. In September, Maisonneuve returned with a hundred five-year recruits.

Amid the terror, Ville-Marie had clung to its missionary raison d'être, instructing, and baptizing the Indians who sheltered there. Murder, arson, and theft were common at Quebec City, but not in Ville-Marie. The settlement's pervading holiness reformed many a recruit; "changed as clothes are after you put them in the wash," Jeanne Mance wrote. Maisonneuve was the final arbiter of civil and criminal cases. He ordered brawlers to pay their victim's medical bills and slanderers to publicly declare each other honourable. He cashiered a soldier for making advances to "decent women" and ordered another executed for "immorality." The soldier was reprieved on condition that he become public executioner at Quebec.

To encourage settlement, resident bounties were offered, and girls were urged to marry young – some even imported from France. By 1664, there were more than 60 dwellings between present-day McGill Street and the Bonsecours Market. The following year, the crack Carignan-Salières Regiment arrived with 100 officers and a thousand pikemen, musketeers and grenadiers under the command of the Marquis de Tracy. In June 1665, he carried the war into Iroquois territory, burning their crops and villages.

In the 20-year peace that followed, the once-austere mission station of Ville-Marie blossomed into the fur-trading capital of New France. Where Maisonneuve had landed in 1642 and where Father Vimont had seen a mustard seed take root, soldiers, merchants, priests and habitants in grey doublets and scarlet sashes, gathered each summer to welcome the great canoe flotillas sweeping down from the north. And as the settlement grew, it gradually acquired a new name: Montreal.

On January 6, 1643, Maisonneuve carried a cross to the summit of Mont Royal, as promised, because the settlement of Ville-Marie had been spared from rising waters. (ILLUSTRATION BY C.W. JEFFERYS)

∞ SIEGE AT THE LONG SAULT

Dollard des Ormeaux, a young man with a shadow over his head, becomes the stuff of legends.

IN THE SPRING OF 1660, a trading party came down the Ottawa loaded with furs from a profitable winter's trapping in the country north and west of Lake Superior. In the van were two young men from Trois-Rivières: Pierre-Esprit Radisson and his brother-in-law Médard Chouart des Groseilliers. As they approached the Long Sault, the rapids above the Lake of Two Mountains, they came upon a large number of Iroquois war canoes abandoned along the shore.

"This put great fear in the hearts of our people," Radisson wrote. "Nor they nor we could tell what to do." Landing a little upstream and moving cautiously through the woods, he sent a scout ahead. Moments later, "he bid us come, that those who were there could do us no harm."

On a small hill, overlooking a clearing littered with shields, war clubs and broken muskets, stood the charred and shattered remains of a wooden

stockade. Every tree around it was riddled with bullets. Everywhere there was evidence of a fierce battle. "It was a terrible spectacle to us," Radisson wrote. But a more terrible sight awaited him; 16 bodies were tied to stakes along the river's bank.

Four days earlier, a Huron by the name of Louis Taondechoren, described as a good Christian but "no soldier," had hurried into Montreal with a chilling tale of what had happened at the Long Sault, a tale of carnage and courage and of the last days of a young French nobleman, Adam Dollard des Ormeaux.

Dollard des Ormeaux had come out from France three years before at the age of 22 with a shadow over his head. Rumour had it that he was seeking a chance to atone for something that had happened in France. It may have been that Dollard himself had talked of the matter or at least had dropped a hint. A friend said, "he merely wanted to be of some use as a soldier."

Soldiers were much needed in New France in 1660. Hundreds of Iroquois were known to have wintered on the upper Ottawa, and hundreds more were camped along the Richelieu. Montreal faced imminent attack. Dollard proposed that he be allowed to recruit a small band of men to make a stand on the Ottawa to prevent the junction of the two forces. Such, at least, is the story that has entered legend. The facts seem to indicate that his plan was less ambitious and consisted of little more than ambushing hunting parties as they came down the river. Sieur de Maisonneuve, the governor of the little settlement, listened and gave his consent.

Across the river in Longueuil, Charles Le Moyne, a wily Indian fighter, and his neighbour, Picoté de Belestre, were not impressed by Dollard's scheme. They argued that a much stronger force was needed, one that must not embark until spring planting was completed. Dollard, well aware that a larger force would undoubtedly mean the appointment of a commander with greater seniority, and convinced that the element of surprise would compensate for his lack of men, refused to wait. Worried that his chance for fame might slip away, he hastily persuaded 16 young men, as eager as he was to risk their lives. After making their wills and receiving the sacrament in the chapel of the Hôtel-Dieu, they set out in mid-April.

Travelling only by night, they paddled deep into Iroquois territory. As few were experienced woodsmen, they lost precious time navigating the treacherous currents around the island of Montreal; a delay that Charles Le Moyne could have saved them. It was a full week before they entered the mouth of the Ottawa. They fought their way upstream past Carillon and the Chute à Blondeau and, on May 1, arrived at the Long Sault.

A short distance back from the rapids, on the eastern side of the Sault, they found an abandoned stockade. It was no more than a rough enclosure of logs, but it was well placed on a hill and offered some protection. A few days later, they were joined by Stephen Annaotaha and a band of Huron and Algonquin warriors. Sixty strong, they settled down and waited.

They did not have long to wait. Within hours, scouts at the head of the Sault brought down word that two Iroquois canoes were approaching. Dollard selected a spot where he thought they might land and concealed his men in the underbrush. As five Iroquois warriors stepped ashore, Dollard and his men opened fire killing all but one. Unfortunately, he escaped to warn the main party.

The next morning, the river filled with canoes. A startled Dollard counted 50, carrying a force of no less than 200 warriors. For the first time, perhaps, he realized the extreme danger in which he had placed his men. He ordered a retreat to the stockade.

The Iroquois swarmed ashore. Not stopping to form up, they stormed the stockade in an immediate attack. Dollard and his men poured volley after volley into them, killing several and wounding many more. The Iroquois chiefs soon realized that a hasty attack would not succeed and pulled their men back out of range. A council was held and unarmed emissaries sent out to parley. In the heat of the moment, the French opened fire, much to the dismay of Annaotaha who told Dollard, "Ah comrade, you have spoiled everything."

Enraged, the Iroquois pondered their next move. They were aware that if any serious delay resulted here they would be late to rendezvous with their fellow tribesmen gathering at the mouth of the Richelieu. Realizing that another frontal assault would be too costly, they set up camp, then moved downshore to smash the French canoes, eliminating their only means of escape.

Dollard and his men set furiously to work strengthening the stockade. They cut down branches to reinforce the walls, binding them around the stakes and crosspieces. They stuffed the gaps with rocks and pieces of sod, leaving only small loopholes from which to fire. A frantic attempt was made to dig a well.

The second attack was launched from all sides. Rushing out from the cover of the trees, the Iroquois attempted to set fire to the walls. The French poured a devastating fire into their closely packed ranks and they retreated in confusion. The Iroquois came back again and again. Each time, they were beaten off with heavy casualties.

Within the stockade, supplies and ammunition were running low. Worse still, Dollard's Huron and Algonquin allies were becoming increasingly unnerved. Renegade Hurons among the Iroquois kept up a constant verbal attack on the defenders, urging them to desert and save themselves while they still had a chance. Dollard succeeded in calming their fears until the seventh day when five hundred more Iroquois arrived from the Richelieu. Ignoring his pleas, every one of them – all but Annaotaha – jumped the walls and ran towards the enemy. Angered and alarmed, he gave the order to fire, and a deadly volley erupted from the stockade, cutting down Huron, Algonquin, and Iroquois alike.

The Iroquois now knew that they faced but a handful of tired men – 17 young Frenchmen and a Huron – odds of 40 to one. Inflamed by their number of dead and certain of victory, they attacked en masse. Hunched behind crudely fashioned wooden shields, they charged across the clearing in front of the stockade as the defenders fired volleys into their ranks. As the front ranks were cut down, those behind stepped into their places, using the bodies of the fallen as stepping stones, until they were at the foot of the stockade. The French fashioned crude grenades by loading pistol barrels with gunpowder and hurling them down on the Iroquois, who were now using axes to hack away at the walls.

Desperate, Dollard set a fuse to a musketoon, a barrel of gunpowder filled with bullets and nails, and attempted to throw it over the walls. Weakened by hunger or wounded, he missed his mark and hit a tree branch. The barrel fell back into the stockade and exploded with deadly effect, killing several of the defenders and wounding the rest. The Iroquois, seizing the opportunity, stormed into the stockade.

In the hand-to-hand fighting that followed, Dollard was among the first to die. All but four of his companions were killed, three later dying of their wounds. The fate of the fourth has never been determined.

Panic set in when word of the death of Dollard and his men reached Montreal. Flushed with victory, it was feared that the Iroquois would now move down river to attack the settlement. But they had paid a heavy price for their victory and turned for home. Their confidence had been badly shaken by the ordeal they had met in carrying a flimsy stockade with no more than a handful of boys behind it.

At the Long Sault, Radisson and des Groseilliers took the bodies down from the stakes and buried them, certain that the Iroquois must have retreated with many dead, "...having to do with such brave and valiant soldiers as that company was."

ABOVE: The desperate struggle at the Long Sault was to enter deeply into the French-Canadian tradition as a singular act of courage that saved New France. (*AFTER HENRI JULIEN/NAC/ C-135-48*)

RIGHT: This engraving depicts those perilous last moments of the battle, when, in desperation, Dollard des Ormeaux set a fuse to a barrel of gunpowder crammed with bullets and nails, and attempted to throw it at his enemies.

✑ MASSACRE AT LACHINE

The fury of a terrible and longtime enemy threatens New France in the late 17th century.

TRAIL-WEARY, HUNGRY, AND thirsty, Samuel de Champlain slept where he fell on the night of July 29, 1609, surrounded by Huron and Algonquin warriors. That night he had a dream. He saw an Iroquois struggling in a lake, crying out for help. As he reached out to rescue him, an Algonquin told him that he was evil and worthless. He turned away and let him drown. His companions interpreted the dream as an auspicious omen.

The next morning Champlain and his Indian allies encountered an Iroquois war party in a clearing near Ticonderoga. He levelled his arquebus and fired, killing two chiefs and wounding a third. "The Iroquois were greatly astonished and frightened," he wrote. "As I was reloading, they abandoned the field and fled into the depth of the forest." With a single shot, Champlain had aroused the fury of a terrible enemy. From that day on, New France would pay a heavy price.

RIGHT: *Although Champlain once shot the treacherous Lachine Rapids, nothing would prove so treacherous as that which provoked the Iroquois into a full-scale attack on Lachine, the bloodiest incident in the colony's history.*

OPPOSITE PAGE: *Iroquois warriors prepare to attack from the trees.* (RECONSTITUTION BY FRANK BACK, CANADIAN PARKS SERVICE)

The Iroquois Confederacy, or League of Five Nations, was the most aggressive and best organized Indian nation on the continent. Initially, the Iroquois viewed the French as little more than a nuisance, interfering with their lucrative fur trade with the Dutch and English. When Champlain irrevocably allied himself to the Huron and Algonquin at Ticonderoga, however, they were transformed from ruthless business competitors to mortal foes, and the Iroquois resolved to drive the French out of the country.

Armed by the obliging Dutch, they launched a reign of terror historian George Stanley described as "one of the greatest offensives in Indian history." Raiding parties ranged from Lake Michigan to the Kennebec, and from Tennessee north to the Ottawa River. The Mohican were almost annihilated, and the Delaware became a subject nation. The Huron, Neutral, and Erie were practically destroyed as independent peoples. "To every point of the compass the Iroquois carried torch and torture," Stanley wrote, "and extended the power of the Confederacy." In 1689, they carried torch and torture to the French.

As early as 1650, the Iroquois had turned their attention to the French settlements, with Montreal and Trois-Rivières being in a virtual state of siege from one year to the next. But the attacks were sporadic, directed at isolated farmhouses, farmers in the fields and the occasional army patrol.

An "infamous treachery" on the part of the Marquis de Denonville, governor of New France, would provoke them into a full-scale attack on Lachine, the bloodiest incident in the colony's history.

In the winter of 1687, Denonville instructed the Intendant de Champigny to invite the Iroquois to a peace parley and "grand festival" to be held the following June at Fort Frontenac. As the preparations proceeded, more and more Iroquois arrived outside the fort to set up camp. On the day of the parley, Denonville arrived with 1,600, troops. Men, women, and children were seized and carried off to Quebec in irons. Forty, including the Mohawk chief Orcanoue, were sent to Marseilles to serve as galley slaves. Then, "unappeased by the atrocities already committed," he ordered a foray into Iroquois territory.

When Louis de Buade Comte de Frontenac, the newly appointed governor, arrived in New France to take up his duties, he brought Orcanoue and the handful of Iroquois who had survived the galleys with him. Frontenac's secretary, noting that they had been released upon order of the King; "the treachery committed being nowise in accordance with his taste." The gesture had come too late.

As Denonville returned in triumph to Quebec, the Five Nations were gathering in great secrecy to plot their revenge. They decided to bide their time until an opportunity presented itself to launch an attack. Word of the planned attack was leaked to the French by an Indian by the name of Louis Ataviata, but his warning was ignored. Denonville refused to believe him, and the Jesuits dismissed him as "a bird of evil omen." As the months passed and the Iroquois failed to appear, the French believed that far from being outraged from their deception, they had been subdued and were about to sue for peace. Philippe de Rigaud de Vaudreuil, the governor of Montreal, allowed the inhabitants who had fled to the safety of the forts, to return to their homes.

On the night of August 4, 1689, in a driving rainstorm, 1500 Iroquois warriors emerged from the mouth of the Châteauguay River and paddled across Lake St. Louis to the Lachine shore. Because of the storm, the sentries on duty at nearby Fort La Présentation failed to see the landing, and the cannon that was to be fired to warn the countryside remained silent. The Iroquois had no interest in the fort and were careful not to alert the garrison. Fanning out to surround the settlement, they waited for daybreak. Then, with piercing war cries, they rushed the houses, setting fires and cutting down those who tried to escape. Many were captured alive.

A survivor recalls that "they displayed every known form of cruelty, surpassing even themselves, and leaving behind them the traces of unheard of barbarity; impaled females, children roasted on red-hot embers, houses burned on every side and cattle slaughtered."

"They burned more than nine miles of territory," Frontenac wrote after visiting the scene. "Sacking all the houses as far as the very doors of the city, carrying off more than 120 men, women and children, after having massacred more than 200 others, who were either brained, burned or roasted, some being even devoured, while the wombs of pregnant females were laid bare to snatch their infants, and other atrocities committed of a shocking and unheard of nature."

Fortunately, the very storm which had enabled the Iroquois to land unseen prevented their crossing beyond Dorval Island, thereby saving many other inhabitants. Terrified, they ran for the forts at La Présentation, Rolland, and Remy. Gates were bolted, a call to arms sounded, and off-duty officers rushed to their posts. At Verdun, 200 regulars were ordered out, under the command of Vaudreuil. They had barely stepped out of their tents when a courier arrived with news that all the dwellings at Lachine were in flames. Marching to Fort Rolland, the troops were astonished at the scenes of devastation. Fifty-six houses had been destroyed and the settlement was littered with charred bodies, many of them bound to stakes.

Vaudreuil learned that a band of Iroquois was encamped in the forests surrounding Fort Rolland. To the dismay of his troops, he refused to attack, reminding them of the Governor's orders to remain on the defensive and "not to risk anything." Undisturbed, the Iroquois broke camp, rounded the island and filed off to the south.

By this time, the troops were "chafing to pursue the enemy." Vaudreuil relented and a hundred volunteers set off. They did not get far before they ran into an Iroquois ambush and were forced to take shelter behind the burned-out ruins of a house. As they exchanged shots with the Iroquois, they noticed a large party of French and Indians from Sault St. Louis and La Montagne marching out from Fort Remy to join them. Helplessly, they watched as they too were ambushed and overwhelmed. More than half their number were burned alive.

The French withdrew to the forts, abandoning the countryside to the Iroquois who continued to carry their attacks to the very gates of Montreal. For weeks they reigned supreme, laying waste to the island and crossing to the opposite shore to sack the village of La Chesnaye, "taking into captivity such of the inhabitants as were not massacred." Only the arrival of Frontenac with hundreds of troops saved New France from being overwhelmed.

So great was the threat of continuing attack, that it was not until a full five years later that the French made a serious attempt to gather up the Lachine dead and bury them properly. Near the ruins of Étienne Lalande's house, they found the skeleton of Jean Fagueret; at another home the remains of Jean Michau, his 15-year-old son, Pierre, and his stepson Albert Boutin. In a hollow at the André Rapin home they found five skulls which were thought to be those of two women, a young man and two children. Other victims were thought to have been burned, their remains totally consumed by the flames. In 1875, a full two centuries later, a farmer digging fence holes uncovered human bones, a knife, and a tomahawk.

The massacre at Lachine did far more than claim the lives of the inhabitants. To their Indian allies, the reluctance of the French to make a stand against the invaders was interpreted as cowardice. "They withdrew with mingled fear and mistrust," Frontenac wrote. "They no longer saw in us those Frenchmen, their protectors, whom they would defend against the whole world. To their mind, we seemed half asleep with our houses burned, our inhabitants made captive, and the best parish of our country entirely ruined."

Champlain's dream had become a nightmare.

OPPOSITE PAGE: *Many 17th century women were neither fragile nor passive as life in New France often presented them with hardships and challenges. Even at her tender age, Madeleine de Verchères was a perfect example of the frontier woman.* (MUSÉE DU QUÉBEC)

❧ THE INCOMPARABLE MADELEINE DE VERCHÈRES

A self-assured schoolgirl saves the day and inspires a people.

THIRTY KILOMETRES NORTHWEST of beleaguered Montreal, the seigneury of Verchères fronted the St. Lawrence extending down river almost to the Richelieu. Flanking the main Iroquois invasion route into New France, Fort Verchères, or Castle Dangerous as it was more commonly known, was home to the Sieur de Verchères, a veteran of the Carignan-Salières Regiment, his wife and family. Throughout the summer of 1692, the Iroquois had been on a rampage, spreading terror throughout New France. Yet, despite the ever-present threat of attack, Fort Verchères was in a state of disrepair. More fort in name than fact, it consisted of a large, stone house surrounded by a crumbling palisade. A curious spell of overconfidence seemed to have invested the Verchères domain. As the season advanced and Iroquois raids became less frequent, life returned to normal. Workers were in the fields harvesting the crops, the seigneur left for duty in Quebec, and Madame de Verchères took advantage of the fine autumn weather to visit friends in Montreal. Only 14-year-old Madeleine, her younger brothers, aged ten and twelve, two soldiers, and an old family retainer named Laviolette remained behind.

On the morning of October 22, Madeleine was on her way to the riverbank to inspect the settlement's boats. Suddenly, a shot rang out and a woman rushed by shouting, "Run, Mademoiselle, run, the Iroquois are upon us!" Years later, renowned throughout New France, she recalled that fateful moment.

"I turned on the instant," she said, "and beheld behind some forty Iroquois running towards me and already within pistol shot. Then, commending myself to the Blessed Virgin, the Mother of God, I ran towards the fort, determined not to fall into the hands of my pursuers. Meanwhile the enemy, perceiving that they were too far off to capture me alive, stood still to discharge their muskets at me."

Running as fast as she could towards the gate crying "To arms! To arms!" she dodged to the right and then to the left as the Iroquois fired. Taking up the chase, an Iroquois overtook her and grabbed her shoulder. Slipping away, she ran through the gate and slammed it in his face. "I hoped," she said with scarcely concealed contempt, "that my call 'To Arms!' would bring someone to my aid; but it was a vain hope."

Instead of coming to her aid, the soldiers left to guard the fort were so overcome with fear that they had retreated to a redoubt where the powder and ammunition were stored. The women and children who had hurried in from the fields were prostrate with grief, mourning the loss of their husbands and fathers, cut down by the Iroquois. Breathless, Madeleine turned her attention to the sorry state of the defences. Fortunately, the Iroquois had not immediately followed up their rush on the gate, perhaps unsure as to how well the fort was defended.

"I gave orders to have the stakes in the palisade replaced," she recalled, "and seized the end of one and urged my companions to give a hand in raising it. After the breaches in the walls had been repaired, I betook myself to the redoubt. Here I found the two soldiers, one lying down and the other with a burning fuse in his hand." When she asked him what he intended to do, he replied that he was going to blow up the fort and its occupants. "You are miserable cowards!" she told them. Taking up a musket, she marched them out to the walls.

Gathering the panic-stricken women and children around her, she quietly and firmly explained to them, with all the wisdom of her 14 years, that they must remain silent so that the Iroquois would not know that they were afraid. They must fight as though they were soldiers, she told them, and perhaps God, who was watching them as she spoke, would send them help. She then fired the cannon, "not only to strike terror into the hearts of the Iroquois, but to show them that we are able to defend ourselves." Shamefaced, the soldiers then her two young brothers opened fire on the Iroquois in the fields. Moving from one firing position to another while the women loaded guns, they were able to create the impression that a sizeable garrison held the fort. The Iroquois retreated into the trees.

For a week, the little band of defenders kept up their brave pretence. They slept at intervals and fired briskly whenever an Iroquois appeared. At night, they paced the walls to keep awake and kept up encouraging cries of "All's well!" at regular intervals. Swaying unsteadily with the weight of the musket she always carried, Madeleine slept little and never allowed them a moment's ease.

On the third day of the siege, a canoe carrying the Sieur de La Fontaine and his family landed at the wharf below the fort. Returning from Montreal, they were totally oblivious of the Iroquois lurking in the trees a few hundred metres away. Alarmed, Madeleine ordered her two soldiers to make a dash for the river bank and escort them to safety. When her order was greeted with silence, she "perceived that they had little heart for the work." Ordering Laviolette to stand sentry at the gate and to keep it open, she told him that if she was killed he was to close the gate and see that the fort was defended "to the last extremity." Then, musket in hand, she "sallied forth to the defence of the party."

"As I expected," she later said, "the enemy believed that this was but a ruse to induce them to approach the fort in order that our people might make a sortie upon them." Reaching the river, she "bade Fontaine land his family, and then, placing them before me, marched to the fort within sight of the foe."

The next day, she went back to the river to rescue her laundry. Clothing, a precious commodity in New France, had been left out to dry before the

LEFT: *In the fall of 1692, the 14-year-old Madeleine de Verchères defended her father's seigneury against an Iroquois party with only two soldiers, an old man and two younger brothers at her side. (PUBLIC ARCHIVES OF CANADA)*

OPPOSITE PAGE: *Nine days after the Iroquois launched their attack on Fort Verchères, Madeleine de Verchères was relieved by men of the Compagnies Franches de la Marine. (ILLUSTRATION BY C.W. JEFFERYS)*

Iroquois attacked and Madeleine was determined not to lose it. When her call for volunteers brought no more response than before, she and her brothers slipped through the gate. Shoulders braced as the defenders fired the cannon for effect, they gathered up shirts and petticoats as the Iroquois looked on with astonishment.

Unknown to Madeleine and her companions, the Iroquois had been completely deceived by the spirited defence of Fort Verchères. They had already lost several men and were reluctant to mount another frontal assault, unaware that they could have carried the fort in a single rush.

As the days passed with no sign of an enemy attack, those within the fort were anything but reassured. The weather was deteriorating, and a northeast gale accompanied by hail and snow began to blow. This, as Madeleine well knew, favoured the Iroquois and she was sure that they "would make a close investiture of the place as soon as darkness set in." She told her frightened little band that by the Grace of God they had been spared another day and then warned them of the likelihood of an attack during the night. "For my part I wish to show you that I am not afraid," she said. "The soldiers will take Fontaine and his family and the women and children to the redoubt which is the strongest place. You have nothing to fear, and I bid you

C.W.JEFFERYS

not to surrender the place even if I am taken, cut to pieces and burnt before your eyes. I shall guard the fort with Monsieur Laviolette, who has never fired a gun, and my two brothers."

Assigning each brother and the octogenarian Laviolette to a corner bastion, Madeleine stood watch in the fourth. Shivering in the wind and stung by hail, they peered out into the darkness. Around midnight, the sentry at the gate warned her that he heard something approaching the fort. She descended from her bastion and joined him, only to discover that the "something" was a small herd of cattle. "My first impulse," she admitted, "was to open the gate and let them in, but, being aware of the tricks of the savages in covering themselves with the skins of animals I determined to wait. After having satisfied myself that there was no danger. I called my two brothers to my side, and each with a musket in hand stood ready to fire, as I opened the gate and let the poor creatures in."

As dawn broke and the storm abated, Madeleine could see that the Iroquois had been busy elsewhere. Columns of smoke rose from neighbouring houses and barns and, in the distance, she could hear war cries. Wearily, she resumed her watch.

The days dragged by, those within the fort growing steadily more worried that help would not arrive. Like the rest, Madeleine was showing the strain. Her face pale and wan, her eyes were shadowed and deep sunken. But never for a moment did she give way to her fears. Early on the morning of the ninth day, she fell asleep at a table, her musket cradled in her arms. Suddenly, she was awakened by Laviolette who reported the sound of movement on the river. Returning to her post, she called out, "Who are you?" Instead of a volley of shots, the answer came back: "Français."

A moment later, Lieutenant Monerie of the Compagnies Franches de la Marine landed with 40 soldiers from Montreal. An ecstatic Madeleine ran to the river bank exclaiming, "Sir, you are welcome. I surrender my arms to you!"

"Mademoiselle," Monerie replied with grave courtesy, "they are in very good hands."

"Better than you think," she replied.

LEFT: *A statuette of Madeleine de Verchères created by Louis-Philippe Hébert.*

OPPOSITE PAGE: *D'Iberville's capture of Fort York followed a brilliant victory over three British men-of-war. The 50-gun Pelican was abandoned after foundering in a storm.*

❧ WAR ON HUDSON BAY

Rivalry between the French and English fur traders brings war to the Bay in the late 17th century.

MÉDARD CHOUART DES GROSEILLIERS was a man with a grudge. Twice he had saved New France from financial ruin only to be fined and imprisoned. Now, taxed beyond endurance, he served the English.

Unscrupulous, crafty and glib, he was the most enterprising fur trader in New France. But, year after year, he had come down the Ottawa River with canoes laden with furs destined to enrich other men. In 1659, he learned from the Cree of a great "Bay of the North," rich in furs, that might be accessible by sea, allowing him to conduct his trade and avoid the predators along the Ottawa. Later that year, he and his brother-in-law, Pierre-Esprit Radisson, tried to reach it by striking inland from the Saguenay. They were unsuccessful, but returned with a valuable cargo of furs to be rewarded once again with fines and jail. On their release, they sailed for England.

Wintering at Hudson Bay was a hardship not taken on by many. Adventurer Jens Munk's drawing represents the winter of 1619 he spent at Hudson Bay.

Wined and dined by London merchants, they were introduced at court. In March 1688, backed by King Charles II and his cousin Prince Rupert, they set sail for the fabled bay aboard the 43-tonne ketch *Nonsuch* and a sister ship, *Eaglet*. Sailing up the east coast of England and into a storm, Radisson and the *Eaglet* were forced back.

But Des Groseilliers and *Nonsuch* crossed the Atlantic then skirted the coast of Labrador, up through Hudson Strait and into Hudson Bay. On September 29, he came upon a river on the east side of the bay which he named the Rupert River in honour of Prince Rupert. *Nonsuch* was hauled ashore and made ready for winter as the crew set to work building a stockade and Des Groseilliers moved inland to contact the Indians. In the spring, 300 came in to trade.

On August 12, 1669, he sailed for home with a fine cargo of furs and proof that the bay route was not only navigable but profitable. The following year, the governor and his Company of Adventurers of England Trading into Hudson Bay received a royal charter giving it power of life and death over its subjects in "Rupert's Land," the right to maintain a navy and make war – and a perpetual monopoly of the fur trade.

The Quaker Charles Bayly was fearless, honest and stubborn – and a prisoner in the Tower of London for refusing to swear allegiance to Charles II. But the Hudson's Bay Company (HBC), sensing in him the qualities needed by a governor, secured his release and, in September 1670, he landed at Fort Nelson – the estuary of the Nelson and Hayes rivers on the west side of Hudson Bay. Moving south, he built trading posts in James Bay, at the

Pierre-Esprit Radisson (standing) and Médard Chouart Des Groseilliers, French fur traders, changed their allegiance between the Hudson's Bay Company and Compagnie du Nord several times between 1666 and 1687, demonstrating the commercial viability of the fur trade through Hudson Bay. (PAINTING BY FREDERIC REMINGTON, REMINGTON ART MUSEUM)

mouths of the Albany and Moose rivers. Indians flocked to them with their furs.

Brandy, tobacco, and muskets attracted them, sometimes in waves of up to 50 canoes in line abreast. To identify an Indian chief as a trading partner, the company gave him a complete outfit of breeches, stockings, lace shirt, plumed hat, and coat with a colourful sash. Before any trading began, the chief and HBC officers sat in solemn silence and smoked a calumet, the pipe of peace and fellowship. With the ceremonial gift of a beaver pelt and the words "Come and trade," a clerk "opened the window," a wicket to the post trading room.

For several days, the posts sold nothing but brandy, fuelling boisterous nights of singing, dancing and fighting. Then, the brandy was cut off and everyone got down to the serious business of trading furs. The Hudson's Bay Company was so successful that it threatened the very existence of Montreal and Quebec.

In desperation, the French formed the Compagnie du Nord and turned to Radisson and Des Groseilliers for help. There was bitter irony here. The French habit of impoverishing them with fines had driven them to England and the formation of the Hudson's Bay Company. But the suspicions of the English and the company's refusal to grant them a share of its profits drove them back into French service. Given the bureaucratic stubbornness of the French and the shortsightedness of the English, there is ample excuse for their conduct.

Scouting the English posts along Hudson Bay, they concluded that they

Trees in the area surrounding Prince of Wales' Fort were cut to heat the stone fort. (PAC/C41292)

were built to "resist the cold and not the arms of those who might attack from the land." In 1682, they took Fort Nelson and a rich cargo of furs. Taxed again on their return, Des Groseilliers retired in disgust to his home in Trois-Rivières while Radisson defected to the English.

Four years later a French regular, the Chevalier Pierre de Troyes, set off from Montreal by canoe with more than 100 men for the south end of James Bay. With him were the brothers Sainte-Hélène and Pierre Le Moyne, Sieur d'Iberville.

Wet, cold and often struggling in water up to their waists, they made their way up the Ottawa into Lake Timiskaming. In a wilderness "frightening in its loneliness," canoes overturned, throwing men and equipment into the icy waters. "Much of our time," de Troyes recorded, "was spent in rescuing each other." They braved portages and forest fires as they paddled into the Abitibi River and down the Moose, cursing the officers and fighting among themselves. "I learned much about the character of the Canadians," de Troyes wrote. "It hardly accords with submission."

By late June 1686, they had paddled and dragged their canoes over 1,300 kilometres and were within striking distance of Moose Fort, a rectangular stockade garrisoned by 18 men. On June 26, d'Iberville reconnoitered the fort, getting close enough to push a ramrod down a cannon to determine whether it was loaded or not. It wasn't, and de Troyes attacked the following morning.

At dawn, d'Iberville rushed through a partially opened gate only to have an Englishman in his nightshirt push it shut behind him, cutting him off from his men. An admiring de Troyes wrote that he "fought boldly with his

Map of d'Iberville's Hudson Bay, 1696. By 1697, several forts and trading posts had been established on the shores of Hudson and James Bays. (MORE BATTLEFIELDS OF CANADA)

sword against all who attacked him." Moments later, the door was knocked down with a battering ram and the fort surrendered, de Troyes castigating the defenders for their negligence, "so great that they had neither guards nor sentinels." By summer's end, he was master of Hudson Bay.

The battle for Hudson Bay continued on and off for the next 11 years. D'Iberville, left in charge upon de Troyes' return to France, spearheaded the French struggle for supremacy. Placed in command of the captured forts, he distinguished himself yet again by capturing two English ships. He took time out in 1690 to lead an expedition against Schenectady (in present-day New York State), then returned to the bay to recapture Fort Albany which had since been returned to the English. During the winter of 1696-97, he terrorized Newfoundland then sailed for Hudson Strait with the 50-gun *Pelican* and three other warships, the *Profond*, *Wasp*, and *Palmier*.

The fleet that d'Iberville led into Hudson Bay was the largest the French had ever sent against the company's posts. Separated in Hudson Strait by fog and ice and a gale that raged for nine hours, d'Iberville sailed on alone aboard the *Pelican* for Fort York. On September 4, 1697, as he sent a party ashore to scout the fort, he spotted three sails on the horizon. Assuming they were the rest of his command, he ordered his crew to "fly the flags of welcome." He was dismayed to discover that the three ships bearing down on him were British: the 52-gun frigate *Hampshire*, the 30-gun *Dering* and the 32-gun *Hudson Bay*. Together, they mounted 114 guns and mustered more than 300 men against his 50 guns and 150 men.

Outnumbered and outgunned, d'Iberville sailed towards them, tersely noting in his log: "Seeing they were English, I prepared to fight them."

Driving a wedge between the *Dering* and the *Hudson Bay*, he loosed broadsides that devastated both vessels. Swinging into line behind the flagship, they returned fire, bringing down much of the *Pelican's* rigging. Nevertheless, she managed to keep the weather gauge and closed to within pistol range of the *Hampshire*. As her gunners frantically loaded, d'Iberville fired a broadside that hit her below the waterline. Almost before he realized what had happened, the *Hampshire*, sails spread and flags flying, was past him and gone – sunk with all hands.

The suddenness of the *Hampshire's* sinking caught the surviving ships off guard. For several minutes, the firing stopped as all aboard the *Pelican*, *Dering*, and *Hudson Bay* "stunned by the gruesome tragedy ... lurched about in apparent stupefaction." First to recover his composure was the master of the *Dering* who fired a final broadside then fled, leaving the *Hudson Bay* to strike her colours. She and the *Pelican* were soon facing a new enemy in the form of a blizzard. Shrouded in tons of ice, both ships foundered leaving the survivors to wade ashore near Fort York. Three days later, they were rescued by the remainder of d'Iberville's fleet and Fort York surrendered; he renamed it Fort Bourbon. For this exploit he was awarded the Cross of Saint Louis, becoming the first Canadian to receive the honour.

Between wars, d'Iberville led an expedition to Biloxi Bay in 1699, establishing the first permanent French settlement in Louisiana. In 1700, he founded Fort Saint Louis de la Mobile, present-day Mobile, Alabama. He fought the Chickasaw in Arkansas and helped build a chain of forts along the Mississippi. In 1706, with France and England at war again, he sailed for the West Indies with a fleet of 12 ships laying siege to and capturing Nevis. Homeward bound, he died of fever in Havana on July 6, 1706, two weeks short of his 45th birthday.

D'Iberville had regained the bay for the French, but it was a hollow victory. Hudson Strait was sealed by the Royal Navy until 1713 when the Treaty of Utrecht returned Hudson Bay to the English for good.

OPPOSITE PAGE: *Pierre Le Moyne, Sieur d'Iberville, became the master of la petite guerre.* (COURTESY MUSÉE DU QUÉBEC)

❧ D'IBERVILLE IN NEWFOUNDLAND

The scourge of Hudson Bay, d'Iberville seems to have set himself the task of removing the English from North America.

"FOR YEARS THE OLD women of the Long House had been gathering wood to burn Charles le Moyne at the stake. Akouesson they called him…"

Or so went the story. Captured by the Iroquois on the Richelieu, they could hardly wait to get him back to the old women. But they were dealing with Charles Le Moyne. Familiar with the Iroquois tongue, he began to tell them of the disasters that would befall the longhouse if they killed him. Whispering and glancing at him over their shoulders, they took counsel of their fears and returned him to his people.

The son of an innkeeper at Dieppe, Charles le Moyne had accompanied Maisonneuve to Montreal and made his presence felt from the start. The first mention of him is found in the Jesuit *Relations* when he was serving as an interpreter with the Huron missions. He became known as a guide and Indian fighter whom the Iroquois came to fear. In recognition of his services, he was granted a tract of land along the St. Lawrence, which he named Longueuil. In 1654, he married Catherine Primot, who would present him with two daughters and 12 remarkable sons, who seemed destined to lead most of the colony's military enterprises.

Charles, their first-born, would succeed his father and develop Longueuil into the most important seigneury in New France; Jean-Baptiste was the founder of New Orleans; Jacques, Sieur de Sainte-Hélène, drove Phips away from Quebec in 1690; and Pierre, Joseph, Louis and Philippe served with Pierre de Troyes in Hudson Bay. Warriors all, his sons would carry the family name into lasting fame.

Pierre le Moyne, Sieur d'Iberville, Charles's third son, was the first great hero in Canadian military history. He became master of "la petite guerre," and seemed to have set himself the task of removing the English from the North American continent. The scourge of Hudson Bay, he had returned to Quebec by way of La Rochelle with a newly-acquired wife and son in the spring of 1696 only to receive orders from the King to move on to Plaisance, the capital of France in Newfoundland.

The French had founded the settlement, now known as Placentia, in 1692 and shared the island uneasily with the English. French fishing villages were scattered along Placentia Bay, while the English occupied the east side of the Avalon Peninsula from Ferryland to St. John's. D'Iberville was now determined to force them out and lay claim to the enormous booty to be obtained from the fishery.

On September 12, 1696, he dropped anchor in Placentia Bay beneath a ramshackle fort with a garrison of 18 men. A day later, a fleet of seven ships with a thousand marines arrived from France. Although the governor, the Sieur de Brouillon, was not anxious to share his authority, it was agreed that he would sail with the fleet for St. John's while d'Iberville and his force struck overland across the Avalon Peninsula.

There were some 35 English settlements on the island, spread out around St. John's and Conception and Trinity Bays. D'Iberville was certain that they could be taken easily once St. John's fell. De Brouillon set sail on October 29, three days before d'Iberville set off with 120 men. Winter campaigning was no novelty to him, but the march across the peninsula became a thing of horror. The route was almost due east, crossing the innumerable small lakes and rivers that mark the head of St. Mary's Bay. When he and his men were not fighting their way through the almost impenetrable forests, they were wading waist-deep in freezing water. All but starving, they arrived at Ferryland nine days later. After putting the settlement to the torch, they marched on to Renewes, where de Brouillon had set up his headquarters.

At Renewes, 80 kilometres south of St. John's, d'Iberville and de Brouillon soon became involved in a bitter dispute about the division of spoils. Before leaving Placentia, it had been agreed that, as d'Iberville had borne most of the cost of the expedition, the greater share of its rewards should go to him. Now, de Brouillon had second thoughts and demanded an equal share. When d'Iberville reminded him of the agreement, the governor drew his sword and challenged him to a duel. Realizing that he was driven only by greed and that he could not take St. John's without him, he agreed to an even split. The atmosphere cleared and d'Iberville proceeded along the coast to Bay Bulls. On November 26, he and his force of some 400 men rounded a headland and came in sight of St. John's.

It had not been an easy march. Heavy snow had fallen, blocking the roads along the shore and horses and wagons had to be abandoned. Struggling through heavy drifts, d'Iberville and de Brouillon were now confronted with a battery of eight guns guarding the narrow harbour entrance and three forts on the landward approaches. Tossing their packs aside, d'Iberville's men charged toward the left of the defenses while de Brouillon drove straight ahead.

Repulsed, d'Iberville and de Brouillon resorted to diplomacy. A settler named William Drew, captured in earlier fighting, was dispatched into the town as emissary, charged with urging the governor to surrender. Drew had been turned over to d'Iberville's Indian allies to be prepared for his mission. According to a contemporary account, the Indians "cut all around his scalp and then, by the strength of hand, stripped the skin from the forehead to the crown." At the sight of him, the governor, unaccustomed to the refinements of French diplomacy, surrendered immediately.

At two o'clock on the afternoon of November 30, 1696, the garrison

The drama of the fleet emerging from the fogs of Newfoundland is caught in this detail from a 1696 map of New France.

laid down its arms and marched out of the fortifications. They were followed by the town's 600 inhabitants. Grandly, de Brouillon offered them two ships he had captured. One would sail for England, the other for France. Those sailing for France would have to find their way home as best they could. After a month of waiting in freezing weather with little shelter and less food, they set sail on Christmas Day.

D'Iberville had given some thought to holding St. John's and making Newfoundland a French colony, but there were not enough men to man the forts. In January, he razed them and burned the town, sparing only two homes that were used to shelter the sick.

With the coming of winter, de Brouillon had had enough of campaigning. Content with his share of 220 captured fishing boats and five million kilograms of cod, he was eager to get back to his comfortable quarters at Placentia. He was equally willing to leave d'Iberville the glory of subduing the country, realizing, no doubt, that there was little glory to share. As a victory over the challenges of nature, the expedition had been an achievement of note. As a conquest, it was pitiful and pitiless.

D'Iberville and his men left St. John's on January 14, bound for Portugal Cove, "across roads so bad that we could find only 12 men strong enough to beat the path." It was early spring when he too reached Placentia, having covered the length and breadth of the Avalon Peninsula and everywhere leaving misery and want in his path. He had taken 700 prisoners and

King Louis XIV of France (1643-1715) ordered d'Iberville to Placentia after the latter's success on Hudson Bay. (NATIONAL ARCHIVES OF CANADA, 2421)

an immense amount of booty and had destroyed most of the settlements and the fishing equipment by which the people lived.

From Portugal Cove he moved on to Harbour Main, a deep and narrow inlet at the foot of Conception Bay. Well up the bay, he attacked Carbonear, which was only saved by the resourceful defence organized by the merchant William Pynne. The settlement became a place of refuge, eventually housing most of the prisoners d'Iberville had taken but was too weak to hold. Baffled at Carbonear, he moved on along the west coast, fringing Trinity Bay by Hant's Harbour and New Perlican to Hearts Content. He destroyed 33 settlements and killed 200 people. He also collected an enormous weight of dried cod – 200,000 quintals or nine million kilograms.

D'Iberville returned to Placentia to be welcomed by five men-of-war lately dispatched from France. They were the *Pelican*, the *Palmier*, the *Wasp,* and the familiar *Profond*. With them came the sixth of the Le Moyne brothers, Joseph de Sérigny, with orders to return to Hudson Bay immediately. So ended a futile, cruel and senseless campaign; a sop to the vanity of Louis XIV and little more.

Months after d'Iberville's departure, an English squadron carrying 2,000 soldiers under the command of Sir John Gibson and Sir John Norris arrived at St. John's and began rebuilding the town. And, under the terms of the Treaty of Ryswick, Newfoundland was formally returned to England on September 5, 1697.

🐌 THE FIGHTING GOVERNOR

Bluff, brave and utterly insensitive to anyone who opposed his policies, Frontenac humbled the Iroquois.

LOUIS DE BUADE, COMTE de Frontenac, was anything but modest. "Onontio," he called himself, "the common father of all nations." When the Iroquois said they would meet him in their council houses, he replied, "It is for the father to tell the children when to hold council." A man of glittering courts and dismal camps, of splendid cathedrals and rollicking barrack rooms, he was always aware of the dignity becoming a high officer for his Majesty the King of France. Frontenac was the grandson of a secretary-of-state and the namesake of Louis XIV. Well educated, he enlisted in the army in his teens and fought in several campaigns during the Thirty Years War. He became the colonel of a regiment at 20 and the equivalent of a modern brigadier-general at 24. When not on active service, he lived at the court at Versailles, running up enormous debts that led a biographer to conclude that "anyone who could borrow that much money

RIGHT: *Sir William Phips and his fleet of 30 ships sailed from England to attack Quebec in 1690. Delayed by fog in the St. Lawrence, he arrived on October 17 and opened fire on the Citadel. Defeated, he withdrew eight days later. (HISTORICAL PICTURES SERVICES, CHICAGO)*

OPPOSITE PAGE: *Comte de Frontenac, Louis de Buade (1622-1698), radiated courage and demanded loyalty. Frontenac was governor general of New France in 1672-82 and again in 1689-98. After suffering much discomfort on his travels, he decided things had to change and he was determined to rule as a mighty lord. In 1673, Frontenac met 500 Iroquois at the mouth of the Cataraqui River in the hopes of establishing trade with this long-time enemy. (DRAWING BY C.W. JEFFERYS)*

from that many people must have had a great deal of persuasive power." At 50, he assumed the governorship of New France and was able to evade his creditors.

When Frontenac arrived at Quebec in 1672, a 20-man guard preceded him down the gangplank. A wide-brimmed, plumed hat covered his thinning hair and his dress and bearing radiated confidence and strength. His military eye immediately recognized that the town atop the cliffs was an impregnable bastion. But he was not impressed with the dinginess of his quarters and headquarters inside the shabby, two-storey wooden structure with the grand name of Château St. Louis. He was even less impressed with the discomfort of his travels on the St. Lawrence to visit the settlements on its northern shores. Much, he decided, needed to be corrected.

Speaking to a throng of citizens gathered outside the Church of the Jesuits on October 23, 1672, he told them that "The Holy Scriptures command us to obey our sovereign and teach us that no pretext or reason can dispense us from this obedience." In a glowing eulogy of the king, he declared that loyalty to him was not only a duty but a privilege, adding: "The true means of gaining his favour and support is for us to unite with one heart in labouring for the progress of Canada."

Bluff, brave and utterly insensitive to anyone who opposed his policies, he was soon involved in a series of violent quarrels with the clergy, local administrators, and the fur traders. His desire for the colony to prosper was also joined by a determination that he should enjoy much of that prosperity himself. Ruined financially, he meant to recover his fortunes. When thwarted, his temper became so uncontrollable that he actually foamed at the mouth. Ignoring instructions from Versailles that his authority was limited, he was

The settlement of Montreal continued to grow as settlers arrived from Europe.

determined to rule – in his own words – as a "high and mighty lord."

While Anne, his long-suffering wife, warded off creditors at home, Frontenac set off for the west to consolidate French control of the fur trade. That trade had been conducted in Montreal in a two-week frenzy of avarice and debauchery. Algonquin, Huron, and Erie had beached their canoes at a muddy common near Place Royale to be greeted by the governor of New France seated in a large wooden chair alongside stalls displaying knives, axes, muskets and clothing. There was much bargaining and bartering: eight knives or two axes might buy one beaver pelt; a greatcoat, two pelts; a musket six. In a courtyard of the Hôtel-Dieu, Indians were treated to a ragout of boiled dog, beaver, bear and corn, seasoned with fruit. At night, drunk on brandy, they roamed the streets whooping, singing, and fighting. Sober, they left with measles, smallpox, and cholera.

Frontenac hoped to pacify and draw the Iroquois into the trade by establishing a post on a small bay where the Cataraqui River flows into Lake Ontario. In 1673, as 500 Iroquois waited, he arrived on the site of the present-day Canadian Land Forces Command and Staff College at Kingston, and set to work building a fort. He was overjoyed, he told them, that they had come "with all the proofs of submission that children owe their fathers." He rebuked them for "treachery and cruelty" toward the Hurons, and exhorted them "to become Christians, by listening with respect and submission to the instructions the Black Robes will give you… to observe strict peace on your part, as I shall do on mine." Goods at the fort, he said, would be traded "at the cheapest rate possible, as I do not intend that you be treated otherwise than as Frenchmen."

The Iroquois watched and listened, hostile to those who had moved into

Quebec under attack from Sir William Phips' English fleet in 1690. The governor's residence, Château Saint-Louis, is visible in the background, where the Château Frontenac, named in his honour, now stands. (PAC/c6022)

territory they wanted to control. For years they had fought the French and their allies, but now, in hard times, they smoked a peace pipe with Frontenac and assured him that they would become Christians as he had urged. They welcomed a trading post on the Cataraqui, they told him, but they pressed for good prices. It was Frontenac's first exposure to the skilled diplomats of the Iroquois Confederacy and he was much impressed, writing to his superior in France that "you assuredly would have been surprised, my lord, to see the eloquence, the shrewdness and the finesse with which their deputies addressed me." But there would be no lasting peace, and New France faced years of mortal conflict with the Iroquois.

Iroquois hostility had actually grown during Frontenac's term as governor. Lulled by their protestations of peace, he had done nothing to strengthen the defences of the colony before his return to France in 1682. His successors would reap the whirlwind. La Barre was recalled after a disastrous series of raids and the Marquis de Denonville stood watch as the Iroquois massacred the settlers at Lachine. Frontenac, now 67 and again in financial difficulty, used his influence to regain the post of governor in 1689, convinced that he could subdue the Iroquois.

His response was to wage "la petite guerre" on the English who made the attacks possible by supplying the Iroquois with arms. English border settlements were raided with Iroquois-like savagery, the French butchering, burning and taking prisoners. La petite guerre raised the morale of New France and awed Frontenac's faltering Indian allies, but it brought about an inevitable response.

In 1690, an English fleet under the command of Sir William Phips sailed for Quebec, determined to destroy the colony. Frontenac received the news in Montreal and headed down river with 300 men, picking up more at every settlement along the way. When told that the English were already at Tadoussac, he sent word back to the governor of Montreal to rush to Quebec with every man he could find. "Vive Frontenac!" the people shouted when he arrived, an old man with fire in his eyes and a sense that this would be his finest hour.

Neither Phips nor few of the 2,000 men in his 30-ship fleet knew the St. Lawrence. Moving cautiously through the treacherous currents around Île d'Orléans, sniped at by habitants along the way, he furled his sails beneath the Rock on October 19 and sent a messenger ashore.

Blindfolded, he was led a roundabout way up the steep streets as the residents stomped their feet and clashed weapons to signify armed strength. Blindfold removed, he was ushered in to the Château St. Louis to behold Frontenac in all his glory. Ever the actor, he had set the scene, and the room was filled with officials dressed for a royal levee, in gold and silver lace, in ribbons and plumed hats, their hair powdered and curled. He demanded that Phips's letter be read aloud. It charged that unprovoked raids against English settlers "put them under the necessity of this Expedition for their own Security and Satisfaction. Your answer, positive within an hour, returned by your own trumpet, with the return of mine, is required upon the peril that will ensue." Frontenac replied: "I will answer your general only by the mouths of my cannon, that he may learn that a man like me is not to be summoned in this fashion. Let him do his best and I will do mine."

Phips's best was not good enough. He landed 1,300 men on the Beauport flats near the mouth of the St. Charles River only to have them bog down in the mud. When he turned his attention to the Rock, a cannon ball shot his flag away as he turned and retreated downriver. Retrieved, it was paraded through the streets of Quebec in a celebration that culminated in a bonfire honouring Frontenac.

Frontenac's victory was followed by one of the worst years in the history of New France. The Iroquois continued to massacre farmers in their fields, and food and wine ran low. Frontenac was afraid that he might be reduced to drinking water. Finally, in the summer of 1696, he mustered a force and marched into Iroquois territory, putting villages to the torch. Exhausted and outnumbered, the Iroquois sought peace. In his 75th year, having achieved what Champlain sought years before, he was borne home in an armchair. He died without riches in 1698, "a true Christian," and was buried in the chapel of the Récollets as a priest praised the virtues that the storm of his life had long obscured.

BELOW LEFT: *The Comte de Frontenac, Governor of New France 1672-1682 and 1689-1698. An avid expansionist, he supported audacious explorers like La Salle. There is no known portrait of this celebrated governor. (NATIONAL ARCHIVES OF CANADA)*

BELOW RIGHT: *The Church of Notre-Dame-des-Victoines in Quebec's Lower Town. Built in 1688, it was given its name in 1690, after the defeat of Phips; the name became plural after the defeat of Walker in 1710. (WINKWORTH COLLECTION, NAC)*

❧ LA PETITE GUERRE

The militia and coureurs de bois excel in defending New France.

"PEACE IS THE DREAM OF wise men, and war is the history of mankind," the Comte de Ségur once remarked. And nowhere was his maxim more apt than in New France, which was almost always at war or preparing for it. A colony in constant danger, war affected every feature of life in New France.

Long before Champlain built his fortress-like habitation at Quebec, five nations – the Mohawk, Cayuga, Seneca, Oneida and Onondaga – had formed the Iroquois Confederacy. United, they had battled the Cherokee, wiped out the Mohican, and humbled the Delaware. They then directed their wrath against the French. Between 1633 and 1701, only 15 years passed when the colony was not subjected to Iroquois attack. Of necessity, the colonists learned to be soldiers, and to fight like Indians, waging "la petite guerre," a war of wile, surprise attacks and ambush.

The spread of New France into the wilderness was resisted both by the

RIGHT: *The Compagnies Franches de la Marine, initially raised in France, came to Quebec in 1683 and were soon augmented by a permanent body of colonial regulars. Although their numbers had increased to 40 companies by 1757, Governor Vaudreuil complained they were chronically under strength by some 250 men. Although some served with Montcalm's regular army battalions, 24 companies of colonial regulars were stationed at Louisbourg during the 1750s. While the men were largely recruited in France, the officers were often Canadian-born.* (PAINTING BY EUGENE LELIEVRE, PARKS CANADA)

OPPOSITE PAGE: *This is the only known contemporary illustration of a Canadian militiaman at the end of the 17th century. In the forests of North America, their ability to dress, travel, and fight in the Indian way made them valuable allies.* (NATIONAL ARCHIVES OF CANADA, C113193)

Iroquois and their allies in the English colonies along the Atlantic seaboard. By the mid-1600s, the English were trading furs at Hudson's Bay and the Iroquois had resumed their efforts to control the trade by attacking the Hurons, French allies in the west. New France now faced conflict on two fronts.

To help defend the colony, Louis XIV had dispatched the Carignan-Salières Regiment in 1665, tough, grizzled veterans of the war against the Turks in Hungary. "Since they have come here," said a priest at Quebec, "we have seen only universal corruption which they have spread by their scandalous conduct." But, welcomed by most, they and their successors often settled in the colony; the officers becoming seigneurs and natural military leaders in times of crisis. Engineers also arrived to build fortifications at Quebec, Montreal and on the fog-bound tip of Cape Breton Island at Louisbourg. Royal funds spent on troops and fortifications became the biggest source of hard cash in the colony.

Nor was the militia neglected. Towards the end of the 1650s, each of the major towns of New France had formed militia organizations sporting special uniforms – white coats for Trois-Rivières, red for Quebec, and blue for Montreal – and every village appointed a captain. In 1669, all men between the ages of 16 and 60 were ordered to drill once a month, the government providing them with blankets, clothing, and a new musket. As Louis XIV had other wars to fight closer to home, the Carignan-Salières Regiment was sent back to France in 1668, except for several officers and 400 men who

Officer and soldiers of the Carignan-Salières Regiment, circa 1665. Reconstitution by Francis Back. (CANADIAN PARKS SERVICE)

remained as settlers. With France's regular army no longer available to serve in the colonies, Jean-Baptiste Colbert, the Minister of Marine and the Colonies, formed a private army, the Compagnies Franches de la Marine, made up of soldiers that had been used to guard naval dockyards. Organized in companies instead of the usual regiments of 1000 to 1200 men, the Marine was formed specifically for colonial service. It was not an elite unit. To keep numbers up and costs down, the Marine enlisted younger, smaller and sicklier recruits. Many were 16-year olds barely taller than the minimum five-foot-five height requirement. Where the regular army and mercenary units generally demanded six years of service from their recruits, Marines had no fixed term of service. Burdened by the cost of sending garrisons off to distant colonies, they were obliged to serve "at the King's pleasure," that is, until the King saw fit to release them.

The first of Colbert's new troops came to New France in 1684 and, within a few years, the original four companies of 50 men each had increased to 28 companies. As Colbert had agreed that commissions in the Compagnies Franches de la Marine would be made available to the sons of seigneurs and other leading colonists, there was no shortage of officer cadets as they seized this opportunity to make the social jump into both the colonial and French aristocracy. The pressure for vacancies was intense, testing the patience of the governor. Few *Canadiens* would join as common soldiers and shiploads of recruits had to be sent regularly from France. A few did guard duty or accompanied expeditions and raids, but most were used as badly needed labourers, the officers pocketing half their pay.

Except for guarding towns, the Compagnies Franches de la Marine was of little use against the Iroquois. Their battlefield skills were not appropriate in the forests where the coureurs de bois and the militia excelled – men who learned to dress, travel, and fight in the Indian way. As a rueful Massachusetts governor admitted: "100 French natives of America, familiar with the woods, able to march on snowshoes and accustomed to the use of birch canoes, are of more value and service than five times their number of raw men newly come from Europe." In small raiding parties, they carried the offensive deep into English territory – Hudson Bay, Newfoundland, New England and the present state of New York – finally bringing the Iroquois to bay. They served New France well until 1759 when Montcalm, ignoring the lessons of "la petite guerre," mustered his troops European-style on the Plains of Abraham.

BELOW LEFT: *Canadian militiamen, first half of the eighteenth century. (RECONSTITUTION BY FRANCIS BACK, CDN PARKS SERVICE)*

BELOW RIGHT: *Soldier in the service of the Company of the Hundred Associates in Canada, around 1650. (RECONSTITUTION BY MICHEL PETARD, DND)*

"A SOLDIER'S LIFE IS AWF'LY HARD"

Conscripts and volunteers, native Canadians, French and British regulars endured hardship and privation to help forge a nation.

WHILE PROFESSIONAL SOLDIERS WERE comparative late-comers to Canada, they have played a significant part in the shaping of our nation. The first "soldiers" to arrive in Canada were either mercenaries employed by the various companies of "adventurers," or freebooters – sometimes "licensed" by their sovereign – who combined the functions of pirate, settler, trader and even fisherman. However, even before the arrival of the Europeans, native Indians developed a complex and effective warrior society. Most males were trained from an early age as warriors, and martial prowess was a key to gaining tribal respect as well as the admiration of the fair sex ("Only the brave deserve the fair" is not a European concept).

Concepts of strategy, military organization, administrative details and use of surprise tactics were all a part of inter-tribal warfare, and later used to

RIGHT: *Between 1653 and 1663, almost 800 French women of marriageable age received free passage to New France along with a priest's certificate attesting to their availability and moral character. Known as* les filles du roi, *plump young women were often chosen first on the basis that they might have the best chance of enduring the harsh Canadian winters.* (HERITAGE OF CANADA)

OPPOSITE PAGE: *In the wilderness, with no medical aid, one could do little but pray.* (FABRIQUE DE LA RIVIÈRE OUELLE)

good effect against the intruders from across the "great waters." Like Kipling's *Gunga Din*, their uniforms were scanty, although some warriors wore a form of wickerwork "armour." War paint and feathered headdress were often added as a psychological measure to terrify their foes (a practise later adopted by European leaders such as Frederick the Great, who capped his already-tall guardsmen with mitred headdresses, so they would appear even taller and, hopefully, demoralize the enemy). The Iroquois even had a system of rank insignia in the form of feathers of different lengths. Armament consisted of bows, clubs, stone-headed tomahawks and, occasionally, primitive knives. Many tribes established effective defensive works to protect their villages.

There was no Geneva Convention in early North America. Captives were tortured, burned alive, or even eaten by the victors. If they were lucky, they became slaves. Scalps were seized as trophies, perhaps because they were easier to carry back than human heads (the Gurkhas, and others, in later years would use the ears of slain enemies to "keep score"). Certainly, the Dorset Indians proved a match for the first European intruders, killing the first Viking leader and later driving the Norsemen to rout with a secret weapon, a large balloon – probably an inflated moose or buffalo bladder – which they hurled into the enemy lines.

In the 1500s, the French arrived. Jacques Cartier's expedition included men-at-arms. Some were signed on especially for that purpose, but many of them were sailors whose duties required them to use the weapons on board when needed. Like their successors, they came prepared and equipped in accordance with European standards. These "soldiers" were actually recruited and paid by the various companies of explorers and traders rather

FAR LEFT: *A French soldier ignites a hand grenade, circa 1688.* (FROM THE COLLECTION OF DAVID MARLEY)

LEFT: *A French musketeer prepares to place his match in the serpentine of his matchlock musket.* (ILLUSTRATION CIRCA 1649)

than by their monarchs. Most of them had seen service, either as mercenaries or as members of royal armies, in the many European wars. Some were "gentlemen-at-arms" who joined the expeditions to seek fame and fortune in the New World. Their dress, equipment, and tactics were those of France and Spain. Metal helmets and cumbersome body armour were *de rigueur*. The effects of these encumbrances in the humid summers of, say, Florida and South America must have been awesome.

The crossbow – first introduced in the Battle of Hastings and later condemned by the Vatican as too barbarous for use against Christians – was being superseded by primitive firearms. The arquebus developed into the musket, which became the principal weapon of the infantry. Early muskets were cumbersome weapons, weighing in at almost 20 pounds and requiring a forked bipod to support the heavy barrel. The English were one of the last European nations to adopt the musket – until 1595 their official weapon was the longbow. The latter was more accurate in skilled hands, and had a far more rapid rate of fire, although the muskets had a far greater stopping power and, no doubt, a greater psychological effect on an enemy. Early muskets were of the matchlock variety. A smouldering piece of saltpeter-soaked cord or rag was attached to the side of the weapon, and, on squeezing the trigger this would ignite the powder in the pan and set off the charge. Until the advent of breech-loading weapons centuries later, these cumbersome weapons were muzzle-loaded. To protect the musketeers while they reloaded (one round per minute was considered a high standard), pikemen were included in the infantry platoons.

RIGHT: *In the mid-18th century, Canadian militiamen wore leggings and moccasins when going on lengthy expeditions through the forest. (RECONSTITUTION BY FRANCIS BACK)*

FAR RIGHT: *In winter, Canadian militiamen in the late 17th century were equipped with muskets and axes and wore thick coats, leggings, and moccasins. (RECONSTITUTION BY FRANCIS BACK)*

Meanwhile, artillery was becoming a science. Often, gunners were comparatively highly paid civilian specialists. Artillery pieces ranged from long guns with ranges of 750 to 7000 yards, firing projectiles of up to 32 pounds, to shorter-barrelled cannon which could hurl a 90-pound shot 4000 yards, to pedreros that fired stone cannonballs, and mortars capable of sending a 200-pound ball over a mile. In New France as in the English colonies, there were few, if any, regular troops. Even the men-at-arms were expected to work as hunters and cultivators, taking up weapons when necessary to repulse Indian attacks.

In the early 17th century, the various British colonies, unlike the French, were more or less autonomous; each colony had its own governor who, theoretically, reported to the Sovereign. Not only were they plagued by the native Americans, they were in a more or less constant state of conflict with the Dutch, Spain, and, often, each other. They had also clashed with their French neighbours from time to time. As early as 1613, settlers from Virginia destroyed French settlements in the Bay of Fundy area – incursions were to be repeated several times in future years.

Later in the century, the battle-lines moved even further north when conflicts between the Hudson Bay traders and the French took place. (One battle resulted in a decisive victory for France's Sieur d'Iberville over a superior English fleet).

At the same time, English and Dutch settlers battled for what is now lower New York state. The Dutch evicted Swedish settlers in Delaware, but, in turn lost, regained and finally lost by treaty their own lands. One

Soldiers patronized taverns for food, drink, and comradeship.
(CANADIAN PARKS SERVICE)

important result of England's victory was the gain of an alliance with the powerful Iroquois, former allies of Holland.

Meanwhile, regular soldiers were few and far between. Although many officials had previous military experience, they were not there as professional soldiers. Only the Spanish, further south, had anything like a sizeable number of troops and even these were inadequate. (The total Florida garrison was less than 300 men.) Accordingly, colonies had to fend for themselves.

In 1638, the Ancient and Honourable Artillery Company was formed in Boston and America's first organized militia unit was created. Even then, many settlers were concerned that the "military" might take over political control. Later, the colony introduced conscription, requiring all males – with exceptions including Harvard students – to undergo a week's military training. Other colonies quickly followed suit.

The British colonies remained at loggerheads – commercial jealousies were aggravated by the English Civil War in the homeland, as well as religious differences. (Maryland, for instance, was predominantly Catholic while most of the others were Protestant; some colonies were loyal Royalists while others supported Cromwell and the Commonwealth.) However, they did get together on some occasions, the most notable being a successful attack on Acadia (again) which had started out as an expedition against the Dutch, and the three-year King Philip's War against the Wampanaog Indians.

Meanwhile, in New France (which had the advantage of the settlers speaking with 'one voice'), a few soldiers were grudgingly provided by the home government; about 100 arrived in the 1640s and were soon distributed in penny packets between Lake Huron and Acadia. Later, small groups of

For minor offences, soldiers were often made to "run the gauntlet" as punishment. (ANNE S.K. BROWN MILITARY COLLECTION, BROWN UNIVERSITY)

reinforcements arrived until, finally, in the 1660s, the first significant unit of royal troops, the Carignan-Salières Regiment, a seasoned unit fresh from European battlefields, arrived in Quebec. The effect of the arrival of over 1,200 troops in a colony with a population of under 4,000 can be imagined. However, they were soon dispersed throughout New France, where they began the task of constructing a chain of forts.

After a few months, the troops, who had adjusted themselves to North American climatic conditions and Indian tactics, went on the offensive against the Iroquois. Following an arduous trek, the 500-man force arrived, not at the Mohawk villages which were their objective, but in Schenectady, which had just passed from Dutch to British control. The troops were compelled to return home, the only fighting being a few minor skirmishes en route.

Eventually, more regulars arrived to assist the French and English. Troops had already been despatched to the West Indies and, with the end of the War of the Spanish Succession, four battalions of the Duke of Marlborough's veterans left for North America. France provided Compagnies Franches de la Marine. These soldiers were recruited in France and actually served under control of the Navy ministry. Their officers were frequently recruited from the younger sons of the "petite nobilité" in New France; indeed, it was a mark of social cachet to hold a commission in the Corps. It also provided career opportunities for "gentlemanly" employment where opportunities were few.

The "bloodybacks" as the British were known (not only from their scarlet uniform coats but also from the frequent floggings which were a common form of punishment) were led in the main by British officers. Exceptions in later years arose when royal regiments were raised in the North

American colonies and officered by colonials (George Washington being one of them). The regular troops came mostly from the British Isles, although it was not uncommon for foreigners to be enlisted to bring units up to strength. Later, in the 18th century, it was common practice for impoverished German princes to conscript young men of military age and hire them out as mercenaries. The British used many of these who came from the dukedoms in the Principality of Hesse, and they were usually collectively known as Hessians.

In Britain and in France, recruiters painted glowing, if false, pictures of military life in order to entice men into the Colours. In England, especially, recruiting quotas were achieved by emptying jails and poorhouses. As the parishes were able to escape the costs of maintaining the poor by passing reasonably able-bodied men to the recruiting sergeants (and, probably, obtaining a kickback for their efforts). Many soldiers were, to say the least, reluctant recruits. Medical examinations were cursory. Many soldiers were illiterate and often, the army was chosen as an alternative to starvation, prison, transportation, or even the gallows. As late as the mid-19th century, over two-thirds of a company of the Somerset Light Infantry had joined the army to avoid starvation.

The French had an unusual practice of allotting *noms de guerre* – nicknames – to their soldiers (this is still continued, but for different reasons, in the Foreign Legion). Many of these nicknames remain today as they gradually became the official surnames of the many soldiers who elected to remain in Canada when their service expired.

French garrison life was not too arduous. After breakfast, those on guard duty took up their places at vital points on the ramparts. Sometimes desultory drill sessions were held, but much of their time was spent moonlighting. Not only was their pay meagre in comparison with civilian workers, but most of it was deducted to pay for clothing, rations and a rudimentary pension fund. A second income was almost a necessity. Sometimes troops would be billeted on local inhabitants (an obligation which met with mixed reception by the townsfolk), in other places barracks were constructed. These were usually crowded, unsanitary and subject to extremes of climate. Food – bread, meat, and dried vegetables – was cooked in barracks by mess cooks for groups of seven soldiers.

Although severe penalties were imposed for serious offences, minor crimes such as drunkenness usually resulted in a few days in the cells. (Their British counterparts would suffer severe flogging for similar misdeeds.) When they could afford it, drinking and gambling were popular diversions. Wine was cheap and apparently moonshine was not unknown. Love, as always, found a way. Many soldiers married *Canadiennes* and settled after their service, a practice encouraged by Paris as the French settlers were greatly outnumbered by the British colonists. For those who could afford it, and were stationed in the cities, "ladies of the night" were always available.

The first French regulars of the Carignan-Salières Regiment were dressed for efficiency rather than looks; brown jackets, slouch hats and equipment more or less carried in the most convenient manner possible. It was not until the 18th century that the standard white uniform, with appropriate adornments, was adopted by France's infantry.

Meanwhile, the British regulars arrived. After a short and abortive effort to quell rebellious colonists in Virginia in 1677, the redcoats left for home. The next significant arrivals were a number of veteran regiments fresh from the European wars, at the start of the following century.

British soldiers in North America lacked many of the advantages of the French regulars and Troupes de la Marine. Their pay remained constant, at sixpence a day, over three centuries. One recruit reported that deductions were made for "washing, mending, soap, hair-powder, shirts, gaiters, shoes, stockings, neckwear, pipeclay and several other items." The remainder was spent on food, and writer William Cobbett states that many men deserted from sheer hunger. In addition, discipline was strictly enforced and floggings were common. Many redcoats who submitted to the blandishments of the recruiting sergeants, or who took the King's shilling as an alternative to starvation, became disillusioned and suicides were a frequent occurrence. As long as the King's troops were in North America, desertion was a problem. Indeed, some recruits enlisted in regiments bound for North America with the intention of deserting on arrival and seeking their fortune in the colonies. In some cases regiments mutinied when, having been assured that they would be sent to North America, they found that instead they were bound for the West Indies, where many regiments lost up to 90 per cent of their strength to tropical diseases.

One thing lacking, perhaps, was the goodwill of the settlers. Unlike the habitants who welcomed the troops as an addition to the work force and, possibly, suitable matches for their unmarried daughters, the British colonists resented the presence of the troops in their midst. Britain's insistence that the independent Americans should pay for their "protection" by taxation aggravated the situation. Indeed, many colonists looked upon their protectors as an army of occupation rather than a defence against the French and Indians.

Unlike the French, whose dress and accoutrements were adapted to North American conditions, British uniforms (and tactics) were reminiscent of the Duke of Marlborough's army. Some commanding officers insisted on their men's *queues* or pigtails being pulled back to excruciating tightness and bound round iron bars, while stiff leather stocks forced the men to keep their heads up at all times. Hair was powdered, usually with flour, which encouraged the presence of fleas and lice; gaiters, belts, and haversacks had to be whitened with pipeclay. The oft-maligned General Edward Braddock (whose lack of appreciation for forest fighting brought on the tragic defeat of two British battalions at the hands of the habitants and Indians at Fort Duquesne) did at least recognize the unsuitability of the traditional uniform, and made some adaptations to North American conditions.

Later, regiments were raised in the colonies, and were armed and equipped in a more appropriate manner. By 1700, the flintlock musket had replaced the unreliable matchlock, while some American units had adopted the Pennsylvania rifle, a much more accurate weapon that encouraged aimed fire rather than the traditional volleys. Dress was less formal and more suitable for the battle areas, while the independent nature of the colonists made for easier discipline.

Following the conquest of Canada, militia units of various types were raised. Some were Fencibles (a shortening of defensible) and were charged with the defence of Canada. The Embodied Militia, recruited from militia units, served for set periods and were paid, uniformed, and equipped like the British regulars, while the Sedentary Militia supposedly trained periodically and could be called out in emergencies. Attempts were made to recruit Scottish Highlanders into a Canadian Fencible regiment (the incentive included discharge in Canada and free passage for their families). Although several Scottish soldiers took advantage of land grants when their service expired, the Fencibles were disbanded following a mutiny in Glasgow, largely resulting from horrendous administrative mix-ups.

Unlike the French, British troops were seldom billeted on the colonists. This was partly mitigated by the fact that limited numbers of wives and children were allowed to join their spouses in barracks. About 30 wives per battalion, selected by a lottery, would accompany their soldier husbands overseas. The rest were out of luck and destitute – there was no marriage allowance in those days. Wives lived in the barracks with as many as a hundred soldiers; a couple's only privacy perhaps a tattered blanket in a corner of the room. The women earned their keep as laundresses, seamstresses, and possibly by "the oldest profession."

Food was perhaps better than the French received, but extras such as tea, vegetables and seasonings had to be purchased from the meagre daily pay. Meat was usually boiled. In some units a "cook" would pull out chunks of beef from the pot, while a comrade would stand with his back to the cook and determine who would get which piece (theoretically this would ensure that everyone had an equal change of receiving the "good" portions). The meagre pay was offset by cheap beer and rum, and drunkenness was common. (The day's rations included an allotment of ale.) As always, "love will find a way," and venereal diseases were a continual problem. Later on, concert parties were popular and, with the support of well-meaning citizens, literacy was encouraged and reading-rooms set up.

Graft was common – at one time colonels were paid an allowance with which to clothe and equip their regiments. It goes without saying that in many cases these grants went into the leaders' pockets, while the men wore threadbare uniforms. In the Regular Army, commissions and promotions were by purchase, and many officers looked upon them as a business investment.

A booklet, *Guide to Officers in the Army*, published in the 17th century, suggested that troops escorting a deserter should sell the prisoner's belongings and purchase ale for themselves, as "he will be flogged anyway." Greedy commissaries made fortunes by selling rotten beef and weevily flour to the troops, who often had no alternative sources of supply.

Desertions were a constant problem. The British deserter had much better opportunities to melt into the local community than his French counterpart. Indeed, The Royal Canadian Rifles was formed specifically to prevent British troops from deserting to the United States. Nevertheless, many redcoats felt that it was worth the risk of a severe flogging, or worse, to begin a new life in the New World. Canada is richer by the legacy of the many thousands of British soldiers (especially the Scots, with nowhere to return to in their homeland following the Highland Clearances) who remained in Canada following their release. Neither can we forget the French soldiers who settled in the St. Lawrence Valley, and whose *noms de guerre* are now respected names in their communities. Their descendants helped forge our nation in Paardeberg, Vimy, Dieppe, and Kapyong. Korea 24-April 195?

LEFT: *A 17th century musketeer carries the accoutrements that made firing a matchlock musket a cumbersome process, unsuited in warfare against the swift and agile North American Indians.*

OPPOSITE PAGE: *The Duke of Marlborough's greatest victory against King Louis XIV's regulars occurred on August 13, 1704 at the Battle of Blenheim.*

🐚 THE WAR OF AUSTRIAN SUCCESSION

In a "woeful decade," France lost much of an Empire and the stage was set for her final defeat.

IN 1700, AT THE beginning of a new century, the future of New France looked bright. The French had weathered a long, bitterly fought war with the English without loss of territory, the Iroquois had been subdued, and they had spread their authority over much of the North American continent. Moreover, their arch-rivals to the south were regarded with something akin to contempt. As an officer in the Compagnies Franches de la Marine put it:

"It is true that this country has twice the population of New France, but the people there are astonishingly cowardly, completely undisciplined, and without any experience in war. The smallest Indian party has always made them flee; also, they have no regular troops. It is not at all like that in Canada. There are 28 companies of infantry, the Canadians are brave, much inured to war, and untiring in travel; 2,000 of them will at all times and in

LEFT: *Philippe de Rigaud de Vaudreuil, governor of New France from 1703 to 1725, had not learned of Port Royal's surrender until the English fleet was already on route to Quebec. (PAC)*

OPPOSITE PAGE: *In 1710, Port Royal was abandoned by Governor Subercase and his men. The following year this port was renamed Annapolis Royal and was garrisoned by detachments from numerous British regiments. (WATERCOLOUR BY JOHN HAMILTON, NAC/c2706)*

all places thrash the people of New England."

During the next half century, this remarkable self-confidence would be severely shaken. In the War of the Spanish Succession – Queen Anne's War to the Americans – France would lose much of her North American Empire and the stage was set for the final defeat in 1759.

Traditionally, the French in Canada were pawns in the larger political, commercial and dynastic games of Europe. On May 31, 1701, Louis XIV – the Sun King – signed a dispatch to his Canadian officials announcing his intention to use New France and the recently acquired colony of Louisiana as a military barrier to block the English from access to the North American interior. This new imperial policy was one element in France's preparation for the War of the Spanish Succession, the outcome of an ill-considered attempt on Louis's part to place his grandson, Philip, Duke of Anjou, on the Spanish throne. Bitterly opposed by England and her allies, Louis's war lasted eleven weary years. At the hands of the Duke of Marlborough, England's greatest general, Louis XIV would suffer crushing defeats at Blenheim, Ramillies, Oudenarde, and Malplaquet. The sun set for Louis in 1715, his prestige shattered and his country exhausted and close to ruin – "a vast hospital" in the words of the gentle Abbé Fénélon, the royal tutor.

In the New World, the time and its tribulations became known as "the woeful decade." Although the Iroquois kept their peace and a new governor, Philippe de Rigaud de Vaudreuil, the first Marquis de Vaudreuil, qui-

etly agreed with New York that there would be no fighting – French furs, blockaded by the British navy, continued to be sold at Albany for a healthy profit – there was no peace with Massachusetts.

In a series of stealthy raids, the French and their Indian allies soon set the entire Massachusetts frontier ablaze.

Hampton, Black Point, and York were attacked by a mixed force of French, Abenaki, and Mohawk converts from the mission at Caughnawaga. The largest raid was against Deerfield in 1704 resulting in 65 deaths. Retaliation was directed against Acadia, the most poorly defended of French possessions. Grand Pré was set afire and Port Royal was besieged by an unruly mob of fishermen and farmers led by Major Benjamin Church, a 65-year-old former Indian fighter who had grown so fat that he had to be levered over fallen trees and hoisted onto his horse. The siege was abandoned after 18 days and Church returned home to be ridiculed as a "wooden sword." A second attack was repulsed in May 1707 and a third later that summer.

All through the years of conflict, leadership had been the one great lack of the English colonists. Individually, they were not without courage and determination, but they had no training in warfare or the leadership of men. They were colonizers – businessmen, traders, and farmers – rather than soldiers. Regular soldiers were denounced by a Puritan divine as "a crew that began to teach New England to Drab, Drink, Blaspheme, Curse and Damn." As well, there was no central guiding force, no common purpose to bring the separate colonies together. There was little love lost between the new aristocrats of Virginia and the Puritans of New England, or between the fishermen of Maine and the merchants of New York – little realization that they must act in concert.

Petty jealousies and divided counsels weren't the only problems. Hit-and-run tactics put all the advantage on the French side. There was little if any defence against the constant raids. In the winter before the Deerfield raid, for example, a force of 600 New England militia had travelled the woods all winter without ever seeing a Frenchman or Indian. The next summer, 1900 men were posted along the border – a ruinously expensive and useless precaution.

Unable to overcome the French alone, the New Englanders turned to the mother country and the Royal Navy for assistance. In September 1710, 36 ships with 3600 men aboard, including a battalion of marines, sailed into Port Royal basin. This time, the attacking force enjoyed such an overwhelming advantage in numbers that Governor Daniel Auger de Subercase and his 150 soldiers, their morale weakened by the ravages of an epidemic, were forced to capitulate. They did so on October 13, marching out of the fort with full military honours, flags flying, and drums beating to be sent back to France. "Honour was saved, but the sight of these starving soldiers in rags and tatters, many of whom were no more than adolescents, saddened even the victors," a witness recalled. The following year, Port Royal became Annapolis Royal, garrisoned by detachments from British regiments.

Philippe de Vaudreuil, Governor of Canada, did not learn of the surrender of Port Royal for several weeks and, by the time he could consider counter-measures, he received word that another English fleet was on the seas, this time heading for Quebec. He also learned that a large land force commanded by Colonel Francis Nicolson, former deputy governor of New York, was assembling at Wood Creek near the head of Lake George. Bolstered with seasoned regulars, this force was to follow the old invasion route into Canada by Lake Champlain and the Richelieu River to assault Montreal.

The concern that swept over New France at the first indications of this two-pronged attack had quickly grown into hysteria. Vaudreuil spoke of "the most bloody war" that was about to overtake the colony and considered giving up Chambly and Fort Frontenac to concentrate his forces for a last-ditch defence on the ramparts of Quebec, but days passed and nothing seemed to happen. Slowly, panic gave way to wonder and then nature intervened.

The fleet that rounded the Gaspé peninsula and entered the St. Lawrence on August 18, 1711, was the mightiest fleet England had ever sent abroad on a single enterprise. Under the command of Admiral Sir Hovenden Walker, it was made up of nine ships of the line and 40 transports carrying seven regiments of regulars with their artillery trains. All that was missing were pilots who knew the river. On the night of August 22, in rough weather, the transports ran aground on Île aux Oeufs drowning 750 officers and men – ten per cent of his total force. At daybreak, a shaken Admiral Walker withdrew the balance of his fleet and set course for home.

At Wood Creek, when Nicolson was informed of the disaster, he tore off his wig, hurled it to the ground, and danced on it in a rage, crying out: "Roguery! Treachery!" Subdued, he burned his fortifications, marched his army back to Albany, and disbanded it.

In Quebec, jubilation reigned. The church in Place Royale in Lower Town was renamed Notre-Dame-des-Victoires. But jubilation turned to dismay with the coming of peace. Under the terms of the Treaty of Utrecht, which ended the war on April 11, 1713, Acadia (the present-day provinces of Nova Scotia and New Brunswick and much of the state of Maine), the vast Hudson Bay trading area and Newfoundland, passed into English hands. In vain, did a French negotiator argue, with cold Canadian winters in mind, that "Canada could be of no use to England, which has no wine to sustain its inhabitants."

This sketch of the village of Louisbourg was done by Captain Ince while stationed there with the British forces. (NATIONAL ARCHIVES OF CANADA/C-5907)

❧ LOUISBOURG, THE MAGNIFICENT FOLLY

Known as the "Gibraltar of the West," the great fortress would never live up to its reputation.

"ARE THE STREETS BEING paved with gold over there?" Louis XV complained. "I fully expect to awake one morning in Versailles to see the walls of the fortress rising above the horizon." Well might he ask, for Louisbourg on the far-off coast of Île Royale was a sinkhole for France's treasury.

Looming over the Atlantic on a narrow point of land at Havre l'Anglais on what is now Cape Breton Island, the fortress was begun in 1720 when Louis was only ten years old and it was still under construction in his early middle age as he lounged in the arms of Madame Pompadour. Year after year, its spires slowly rose out of the sea mists, a seemingly impregnable bastion meant to safeguard the heartland of New France. Year after year, too, officials embezzled money earmarked for its construction, and the costs of labour and building materials shipped from France continued to

RIGHT: After the Treaty of Utrecht in 1713 the French founded Louisbourg. This fortified town became a bustling seaport which often came under fire. (PAC/NAC 27651)

OPPOSITE PAGE: View of the port and town of Louisbourg in August 1744. Reconstitution by Lewis Parker. (FORTRESS LOUISBOURG, CANADIAN PARKS SERVICE)

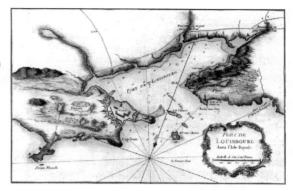

soar. Walls bulged, stones cracked and mortar melted away. More expensive than Pompadour, it would eventually drain his treasury of 30 million livres.

Known as the "Gibraltar of the West," the fortifications at Louisbourg were based upon the principles of defence developed by the renowned military engineer, Le Prestre de Vauban. They eventually enclosed a town area of some 57 acres with 30-foot-high masonry walls and a series of bastions bristling with 148 cannon. Smaller ramparts and gun emplacements guarded the entrance to the harbour. Marshes, Micmac Indians who were paid a livre apiece for enemy scalps, a glacis, ditch and covertway provided additional protection on the landward side.

Graced with a slender tower, the King's Bastion was Louisbourg's administrative and military centre and contained the governor's apartments, a chapel, officers' rooms, and quarters for the garrison. The town boasted two dozen inns and taverns, shops, brothels, a theatre, an icehouse, a hospital and a convent school. Rich and poor lived crowded together around the town. Commercial warehouses brimming with rum, sugar and tobacco from the West Indies abutted homes and public buildings and soldiers relaxed in taverns adjacent to the residences of the rich. The harbour was filled with fishing shallops and merchantmen. Fortress, and commercial centre, the cobblestone streets teemed with soldiers and sailors, merchants, fishermen, and bewigged royal officials and their ladies holding perfumed handkerchiefs to their noses as the breeze carried the reek of drying codfish across the town. The population waxed and waned by the season, reaching 4000 by mid-century.

The garrison, a mixed force of Compagnies Franches de la Marine and Swiss mercenaries, detested Louisbourg, cursing its isolation and perpetual fog. "A hideous country ...the most stony of any place on earth," one soldier called it. The common soldiers were treated abominably. Poorly paid and fed, they lived in unheated quarters so verminous that in summer they slept on the ramparts. Drunkenness was endemic. Officers, already surreptitiously trading wine and luxury goods to New England merchants, were granted the exclusive right to sell liquor and took a cut of the profits of taverns and brothels. Reduced to selling pieces of equipment on the black market or taking part-time civilian jobs on the fortifications, the troops were driven to mutiny in 1744 when a bibulous governor neglected to lay in sufficient provisions for the winter.

For years, New Englanders had looked upon Louisbourg with growing concern, but it took the outbreak of King George's War – part of the larger European War of Austrian Succession – to underscore the threat the fortress posed. French privateers began to operate out of Louisbourg, preying on coastal trade and seizing fishing boats. Annapolis Royal was attacked and, in May 1744, the settlement of Canso at the mouth of Chebucto Bay was captured and the garrison carried off to the fortress – a fatal error since this gave the English the opportunity to study its defences. The French gained little by the attacks. As one Louisbourg resident said: "The English might never have troubled us had we not affronted them first ...The inhabitants of New England wanted to live in peace with us. They would no doubt have done so had we not ill-advisedly deprived them of that security they felt toward us."

Despite Benjamin Franklin's warning that "fortified towns are hard nuts to crack, and your teeth are not accustomed to it," a rag-tag force of volunteers under the command of William Pepperell, a Boston lumberman, set sail for Louisbourg in April 1745 aboard a hastily-improvised flotilla of coastal traders and fishing vessels. Clerks, fishermen, farm boys, and students, few had any military experience. Cold and seasick, they met little resistance as they scrambled ashore in Gabarus Bay south of the town, dragging their cannon through the surf. Offshore, British warships blockaded the harbour under Sir Peter Warren, one of the first Englishmen to have a dim inkling of the fact that colonists could fight.

Undaunted by the reputation of the famous fortifications, more than 2000 were soon ashore, setting up cannon on hillocks from which they

TOP AND FAR LEFT: *Although they were only 40 feet long and crudely built, Viking longships were incredibly seaworthy. Intrepid Norse explorers are believed to have "discovered" Newfoundland and Labrador circa 1000 A.D. When trouble arose between Norse settlers and the Native Dorset peoples, the weapons of the Vikings – metal axes, armour, swords, spears and wooden shields – proved to be inferior to the natives' primitive bows and arrows combined with the Dorsets' hit and run tactics.* (BOTH PHOTOS: RECONSTITUTIONS BY LOUIS S. GLANZMAN, NATIONAL GEOGRAPHIC SOCIETY)

ABOVE: *This decorative bowsprit (inset right) adorned the bow of a drakkar. These dragon heads, sculpted in wood, were meant to terrify those attacking the Viking longships.*

LEFT: The custom of removing an enemy's scalp dates back some 2500 years to the Scythians of southern Russia. It was the early Europeans who came to North America who introduced scalping to the native tribes. They also offered payment upon receipt of scalps as proof of death. To the Amerindian, scalping was the white man's custom. (LIBRARY OF CONGRESS)

BELOW: As many as 20 Spanish Basque ships sailed for the coast of Labrador to hunt whales each spring, departing before the winter ice formed. Settlements were seasonal only, unless the misfortune of lost ships forced some sailors to remain over the winter. (PAINTING BY RICHARD SCHLECHT, NATIONAL GEOGRAPHIC SOCIETY, WASHINGTON)

TOP: *During Martin Frobisher's expedition to Baffin Island in northern Canada in 1577, relations rapidly deteriorated between the Inuit and the English. This culminated in the Battle of Bloody Point, the first to occur in the north.* (WATERCOLOUR BY JOHN WHITE, TRUSTEES OF THE BRITISH MUSEUM)

ABOVE: *Most Amerindian tribes established fortifications around their towns and villages. Although gone by the time Europeans arrived, pre-Columbian tribes established large settlements such as Cahokia (near present-day Collinsville, Illinois), population 20,000. Towns such as Cahokia, pictured below circa 1200 A.D., thrived with markets and river ports in and around them.* (RECONSTITUTION BY MICHAEL HAMPSHIRE, CAHOKIA MOUNDS STATE HISTORIC SITE, ILLINOIS)

ABOVE: *Champlain (in red) had allied the French with the Algonquin and Huron tribes against the Iroquois. In this depiction he is bidding farewell to the first coureur de bois, Étienne Brûlé. Departing on a dangerous journey with 12 Huron warriors, Brûlé travelled through Iroquois territory to enlist the aid of the Susquehannahs. Anxious for battle, Champlain refused to wait for Brûlé and the Susquehannahs to arrive before launching his attack in October 1615. Wounded in battle, Champlain would be forced to admit defeat in the face of a strongly defended fort. Brûlé and his allies would arrive nine days later.* (PAINTING BY REX WOODS, NEW YORK HISTORICAL SOCIETY)

FAR LEFT: *This engraving depicts the perilous last moments of the May 1660 Battle of Long-Sault, when Dollard des Ormeaux set a fuse to a barrel of gunpowder crammed with bullets and nails, and attempted to throw it at his enemies. (ENGRAVING PUBLISHED IN "LA NOUVELLE-FRANCE," HACHETTE 1904)*

ABOVE: *British soldiers occupying Port Royal and Quebec between 1629-1632 probably dressed similarly to these musketeers. (RICHARD CATON-WOODVILLE, BROWN UNIVERSITY)*

RIGHT: *By 1680, there were some 600 coureurs de bois who lived in the forests of New France. Many adopted buckskins and the ways of the Indians and made their living by trading furs and acting as valuable interpreters for the French. (ALAIN BIENVENUE)*

ABOVE: *Pierre-Esprit Radisson (standing) and Médard Chouart, Sieur Des Groseilliers, French fur traders, changed their allegiance between the Hudson's Bay Company (HBC) and Compagnie du Nord several times between 1666 and 1687, demonstrating the commercial viability of the fur trade through Hudson Bay.*
(PAINTING BY FREDERIC REMINGTON, REMINGTON ART MUSEUM)

LEFT: *Trade between the Indians and HBC always began with solemn ceremony. The Indians arrived in canoes, sometimes as many as 50 abreast. A parade ensued and the Indian chief would be clothed in English finery provided by the HBC. (In this depiction, he is in the background wearing one red and one green legging.) A company officer would call out "come and trade," the chief replying "open the window." For two or three days, the fort sold only brandy. Indian and HBC leaders then met again to trade furs for brandy, tobbacco, muskets and food.*
(HUDSON'S BAY COMPANY)

ABOVE: Brothers Louis-Joseph and François de La Vérendrye did not reach the "Western Seas," but discovered the Rocky Mountains in January 1743. Believing they were insurmountable, the brothers turned back. The Pacific Ocean would not be reached by overland expedition until July 1793, when explorer Alexander Mackenzie reached the mouth of the Bella Coola River. At its zenith, French territory extended from Saskatchewan to Cape Breton and down to the Gulf of Mexico. (CHARLES W. JEFFERYS, ART GALLERY OF ONTARIO)

RIGHT: The Battle in the Bay, on September 5, 1697, saw Pierre Le Moyne d'Iberville in the 44-gun Pelican (right) battle HMS Hampshire for control of Hudson Bay and its fur trade. (PAINTING BY NORMAN WILKINSON)

ABOVE: *Having lost Louisbourg to the French, Lieutenant Colonel the Honourable Edward Cornwallis, established the fortified town of Halifax two miles inland from the inlet of Chebucto in June 1749. Within a week, 13 ships and more than 2500 settlers arrived, attracted by the promise of a year's free rations. By winter, more than 3000 houses had been constructed, and by the following September, the first Protestant Church in Canada, St. Paul's, held its inaugural service.* (C.W. JEFFERYS, ART GALLERY OF ONTARIO)

LEFT: *An illustration of Ottawa war chief Pontiac taking up the hatchet in 1763. Abandoned by their French allies, defeated and despised, the Native tribes of the northwest rallied around the little-known Ottawa chief. Pontiac would lead the attack on Fort Detroit, but his coalition of tribes quickly abandoned him.* (GRANGER COLLECTION)

ABOVE: When the Treaty of Utrecht was signed in 1713, the land known as Acadia became a British possession. The Acadians, predominantly French-speaking Roman Catholics, had strived to maintain their neutrality in political matters. However, in 1755, their promise of neutrality was seen by the British government as an unwillingness to fight the enemy at a time when the struggle for control of North America was intensifying. Under pressure to act, the lieutenant-governor of Nova Scotia, Colonel Charles Lawrence, decided that the Acadians posed too great a threat to British security and ordered their expulsion. Between 1755 and 1763, some 10,000 men, women and children were forced to abandon their lands. The Acadians were deported to several British colonies along the eastern seaboard, some settling as far south as Louisiana. After 1763, Acadians were allowed to return to their homelands, and by 1764 were once again permitted to own land in Nova Scotia. By 1800, their population had reached 8000 in Canada. (PAINTING BY CLAUDE PICARD)

RIGHT: Comte de Frontenac defended Quebec City from the English in 1690. (PUBLIC ARCHIVES OF CANADA)

ABOVE: In 1755, General Edward Braddock was shot from his horse while on his way to attack Fort Duquesne. His second-in-command, 23-year-old George Washington, led a beaten army back to Great Meadows. (WISCONSIN STATE HISTORICAL SOCIETY)

LEFT: William Pitt (the Elder), 1st Earl of Chatham (1708-78). Prime minister of Britain from 1756-61 and 1766-68, he brought the Seven Years War to a successful conclusion in Canada. Under Pitt, the war in Canada would no longer be just about fur; it would also be about territory and a settling of scores with the French dating back to Champlain's time. Pittsburgh, Ohio, the former Fort Duquesne at the junction of the Alleghany and Monongahela rivers, was named in his honour. (GRANGER COLLECTION)

ABOVE: *Panoramic view of Louisbourg in August 1744. Founded in 1713, the fortified capital of Île Royale (present-day Cape Breton Island) was established in the same year that France ceded Newfoundland and Acadia to Britain according to the terms of the Treaty of Utrecht. With a population of 4000, Louisbourg quickly became an important port and strategic military centre with a permanent garrison of 1700 soldiers. The town came under siege in 1745 and 1758, and on both occasions was forced to capitulate. The fortress of Louisbourg is now a national historic site. (LEWIS PARKER, CANADIAN PARKS SERVICE)*

RIGHT: *Pierre de Rigaud de Vaudreuil, the son of the governor who had led New France early in the 18th century, became governor general himself in 1755. A Canadian by birth, Vaudreuil knew the importance of maintaining alliances with the Native peoples. (PAC)*

ABOVE: *Cannoniers-bombardiers manoeuvering an artillery piece into place in the mid-18th century. The gun is representative of the type of artillery found in the forts of New France.*
(RECONSTITUTION BY EUGÈNE LELIÉPVRE)

LEFT: *Canadian militiamen in their winter dress, toward the end of the 17th century.*
(RECONSTITUTION BY FRANCIS BACK)

TOP: *Scots of the Black Watch advance against the French defences at Carillon, but without effective artillery support they were slowed by Montcalm's abatis. Determined to break the French line, they attacked repeatedly despite appalling casualties.* (ANNE S. K. BROWN MILITARY COLLECTION)

ABOVE: *In 1673 Governor Comte de Frontenac went to Cataraqui to establish a new inland base at the foot of Lake Ontario, where future Kingston would grow. He liked to travel in style and devised a special chair to accommodate travel by canoe.* (J.H. DE RINZY, NATIONAL ARCHIVES OF CANADA)

On July 31, 1759, General James Wolfe made his first serious assault on the French positions at Montmorency, near Quebec City. Scaling the cliffs by the waterfall, his troops would be cut down by General Montcalm's men, and he would order a retreat. A month and a half later, it would be a different story. On September 13, Wolfe ordered Lieutenant Colonel William Howe and his advance party of Scottish Highlanders to scale the cliffs above the Anse de Foulon and take the small outpost at the edge of the Plains of Abraham. Seizing the position, Howe signalled Wolfe. Within minutes, hundreds of redcoats joined them on the heights. (ILLUSTRATION BY HENRY SANDHAM)

ABOVE AND RIGHT: *"The Death of General Wolfe, Quebec." Receiving the all-clear from William Howe, Major General James Wolfe and the rest of his 4440-strong army scaled the cliffs at the base of the Plains of Abraham as Admiral Charles Saunders' warships continued their steady bombardment of Quebec. On the morning of September 13, 1759, General Louis de Montcalm gathered his 4500 troops to meet Wolfe's. The French army lost not only the battle, but also lost its leader, as Montcalm was fatally wounded in the skirmish. As the British advanced, Wolfe was hit three times, the last shot piercing his chest as his aides and an Indian warrior rushed to his side. Wolfe, who would be immortalized for his victorious campaign, was one of only 58 British fatalities in the final battle at the Plains of Abraham.*
(*PAINTING BY ALONZO CHAPPEL, NAC/C-042249*)

TOP: *Halifax, Nova Scotia, in 1780. The Union Jack flies above the wooden palisades of the first* citadel. (PUBLIC ARCHIVES OF CANADA)

ABOVE: *A fanciful depiction of the death of General Montcalm, who died at daybreak the day after the battle on the Plains of Abraham. He was buried near the Ursuline convent. In 2001, Montcalm's remains were moved in a solemn procession to the cemetery of the General Hospital, where he was reburied among his soldiers.*

could fire into the fortress. Others, harnessed together like oxen, manhandled their guns through the marshes then opened fire from the high ground behind Louisbourg. A group of French officers shouted insults and stood on the walls raising wine glasses in mock toasts until a cannon ball smashed into them, killing 14. Counter-battery fire from the fortress decapitated a gunner and gutted his mate. Appalled, one New Englander wrote of his first taste of war: "It is an awful thing to see men wounded and wollowing in their own blud and breething oute their last breths." The bridgehead secure, Pepperell landed the rest of his force the next morning.

Governor Louis Duchambon abandoned the outer works and withdrew his men into the fortress. Unfortunately, the guns of the Grand Battery which dominated the harbour had not been properly spiked, and within hours the New Englanders were using them to batter the Dauphin Gate. "The enemy saluted us with our own cannon," a soldier recalled, "and made a terrific fire, smashing everything within range." Inexperience sometimes led them to overcharge the guns, blowing the barrels and killing or maiming the crews. Day after day they blasted the walls. "Never was a place so mauled with cannon and shell," Pepperell said, noting that the town was hit by over 9000 cannon balls and 6000 bombs.

The destruction was tremendous, the once elegant streets and squares of the town were pounded into rubble as civilians cowered in basements and bomb shelters. Cannon balls with hissing fuses rolled down the cobblestones and mortars exploded overhead showering death and destruction below. Not a single building remained intact. A lucky gunner shot away the bell in the citadel tower, the Marine offices on the quay collapsed alongside inns, shops, and homes. Morale, already shaky after the previous year's mutiny, hit bottom when the *Vigilante*, heavily laden with supplies for the garrison, was captured by Warren's fleet.

On June 27, after a seven-week bombardment, the French surrendered. With flags flying and muskets shouldered, Duchambon and his men marched out of the "impregnable bastion" and the New England militia marched in. François Bigot, the corrupt Intendant, left with the royal treasury of some four million livres among his "personal possessions." England and New England celebrated with ringing church bells and booming artillery salutes. Pepperell was knighted and Warren promoted. Three years later, their victory, "the people's darling conquest – the greatest Conquest that Ever was Gain'd by New England," was betrayed. Under the terms of the Treaty of Aix-la-Chapelle, Louisbourg was returned to France in exchange for a trading post in India.

An ungrateful, untrustworthy England had swapped Louisbourg "for a trumpery factory in Madras."

BELOW: *Supported by the British navy, Sir William Pepperell and his New England troops land at Louisbourg.* (PAINTING BY J. STEVENS, NAC/C10994)

OPPOSITE PAGE: *Unable to continue the journey to the "western sea," Pierre Gaultier de La Vérendrye sent his sons, Louis-Joseph and François, west. On January 8, 1743, they reached the Rocky Mountains.* (ILLUSTRATION BY C.W. JEFFERYS)

ꙮ THE WAY WEST

*La Vérendrye and his sons, their
imaginations fired by tales of vast plains
stretching out to a western sea, set out in
1730 on a journey of exploration.*

CHAMPLAIN MIGHT URGE the settlers at Quebec "to cultivate the land before all things," but life on the land held little appeal for
adventuresome young men, particularly when there were fortunes to be
made in the fur trade. As *coureurs de bois*, they would range the continent,
opening up a vast commercial empire. Missionaries too, in their singular
devotion to convert the Indians to Christianity, would penetrate into re-
gions never before travelled by Europeans.

Interest in Canada had been sparked by Champlain's writings and by
Gabriel Sagard's *Le Grand Voyage au Pays des Hurons*. But it was the Jesuit
Relations, the annual report of the order's activities, which aroused widespread support for their work and encouraged immigration. "Why cannot
the great forests of New France largely furnish the ships for the Old?" the

report for 1636 asked. "Who doubts that there are mines of copper and other metals? ... All those who work in wood and iron will find employment here."

Étienne Brûlé was the first coureur de bois. Born of French peasant stock, he was among the first settlers at the Habitation at Quebec. But the forests beckoned and Champlain, eager for information about the lands to the west, granted his request to travel to the Huron country. From then until his death in 1633, he lived among the Indians, learning their languages and adopting their customs. He was the first white man to see lakes Ontario, Erie, Huron, and Superior and may have made his way into Lake Michigan. He was followed by Jean de Brébeuf and his Jesuit brethren who settled at Sainte-Marie among the Hurons near present-day Midland on Georgian Bay. Martyred in 1649 when the Iroquois destroyed Huronia, Brébeuf's work was taken up by the priest Jacques Marquette and merchant Louis Joliet who explored the routes leading into the Mississippi and travelled down the great river to within 700 miles of the Gulf of Mexico.

Pierre-Esprit Radisson and his brother-in-law, the self-styled Sieur Médard Chouart Des Groseilliers, were the first fur traders in the Lake Superior region. Twice they had saved New France from financial ruin only to be imprisoned and fined for leaving the colony without the governor's permission. Disgusted, they offered their services to the King of England and extended the fur trade into Hudson Bay.

The fur trade attracted René-Robert Cavelier, Sieur de La Salle as well, but only as a means to finance his quest for a route to the Orient. In 1678, with 30 men and the blessing of Louis XIV, he set out to claim the Great Lakes and the Mississippi River for France. On Lake Erie, he built the 45-ton *Griffon*, the first ship to be launched on the Great Lakes. Forced to return to Quebec when the *Griffon* foundered with a load of furs, he organized a new expedition in 1681 and followed the Mississippi to its mouth. On 9 April 1682, he raised a cross bearing the arms of France in an alligator-infested swamp and claimed the land, which he named Louisiana. Three years later, he returned by sea with a band of settlers raked up from the poorhouses and prisons of France. Landing in Galveston Bay, he set off overland only to be murdered by his men who could no longer bear his haughty manners.

Pierre Gaultier de La Vérendrye was a much more congenial man. An obscure officer lacking in means despite his brilliant service record, he was stationed at Kaministigoyan near Thunder Bay when he heard the Indians speak of vast plains stretching out to a western sea. His imagination fired, he set out on a journey of exploration in 1730 with his sons and a small band of cadets of the Compagnies Franches de la Marine. Realizing that he would have to trade with the Indians in order to finance his expedition, he left a string of forts and alliances in his wake. Exhausted, he was forced to return home the following year, leaving his sons, Louis-Joseph and François, to continue the explorations alone. Joined by a procession of hundreds of curious Indians, they advanced slowly across the plains and reached the Rockies on January 8, 1743. Fourteen months later, they were reunited with their father at Fort La Reine.

By the mid-18th century, French possessions reached from Cape Breton Island to the Rockies and from the Great Lakes to the Gulf of Mexico. In time, across this vast land, a sense of nationhood would be born.

Jacques Marquette (1637-1675), a French Jesuit missionary, and Louis Jolliet (1645-1700), born in Quebec, were sent to explore the Mississippi River. (PUBLIC ARCHIVES OF CANADA)

❧ MORE THAN A SIDESHOW

Determined to crush the French regime in Canada, Pitt concentrates his forces in North America… A century-old rivalry is about to come to an end.

THERE WERE RUMBLINGS OF mutiny at Louisbourg in the winter of 1745. The thrill of victory had passed and morale collapsed as the triumphant New Englanders were committed to the dull labour of repairing walls and buildings and removing accumulated filth from the streets. Disease ravaged the garrison with no fewer than 2000 men dying before the arrival of spring weather. In the years to come, it would prove as unpopular a posting as it had been to French regulars and Swiss mercenaries. Still, it was with a sense of outrage that they learned that the fortress was to be returned to France under the terms of the Treaty of Aix-la-Chapelle.

The War of the Austrian Succession had changed nothing and settled nothing. Both France and England were too much absorbed with the bal-

RIGHT: Looking southeast over one-fifth of reconstructed Louisbourg, the Dauphin Gate is visible in the foreground.
(FORTRESS LOUISBOURG, CANADIAN PARKS SERVICE)

OPPOSITE PAGE: No longer a sideshow, the struggle for the new continent grew. While the grounded warship Prudent *erupts in flames, British boarding parties sail the* Bienfaisant *out of the harbour at Louisbourg on June 2, 1758. (METRO TORONTO REFERENCE LIBRARY, MTL 2653)*

ance of power in Europe to be concerned with a sideshow on a fog-bound, faraway shore. Pawns of the imperial powers, the century-old rivalry between the French and English in North America would continue with the ever-growing conviction that, ultimately, one or the other must prevail. All the encounters till now were only a prelude to an inevitable final trial of strength. The prize was a continent.

The French greatly improved the defences of Louisbourg and sent out 1500 troops under officers who this time maintained discipline. Merchants and fishermen with their families re-established themselves; the fishery expanded rapidly and the old trade with Canada, the West Indies, and New England flourished. By 1752, the population stood at 5845. Old alliances with the Micmac and Abenaki were revived and Acadians were encouraged to settle on Île Royale, Île St. Jean, and around the French fort at Beaubassin. As always, they were to be the victims of deals and wars they had no hand in starting and no power to stop.

Although Britain compensated the New Englanders for the costs of the Louisbourg expedition, the colonists were not pacified. Once again, the fortress threatened their shipping and North Atlantic trade. A generation later, their bitterness and sense of betrayal would fuel the American Revolution. Louisbourg has aptly been called "the cradle of the United States."

War would not be declared again until May 1756. In the meantime, the struggle went on as the French attempted to check English expansion championed by powerful commercial interests led by the Duke of Newcastle, the Earl of Halifax, and Lord William Pitt, planters and land speculators in the American colonies. It was a struggle in which the French seemed to have all the advantage. As a contemporary American observer put it:

"Our colonies are all open and exposed, without any manner of security or defence. Theirs are protected and secured by numbers of forts and fortresses. Our men in America are scattered up and down the woods, upon their plantations, in remote and distant provinces. Theirs are collected together in forts and garrisons. Our people are nothing but a set of farmers and planters, used only to the axe or hoe. Theirs are not only well trained and disciplined, but they are used to arms from their infancy among the Indians; and are reckoned equal, if not superior in that part of the world to veteran troops.

"Our people are not to be drawn together from so many different governments, views, and interests; are unwilling, or remiss to march against an enemy, or dare not stir, for fear of being attacked at home. They are all under one government, subject to command like a military people. While we mind nothing but trade and planting. With these the French maintain numbers of Indians – We have none – These are troops that fight without pay – maintain themselves without stores and magazines – we are at immense charges for those purposes. By these means a few Indians do more execution, as we see, than four or five times their number of our men, and they have almost all the Indians of that continent to join them."

"Our strong point is to attack," said Governor La Galissonière, the recently appointed Governor of New France. "It is the only way to have nothing to fear here. Inaction will preserve nothing. If we do not attack we will be attacked and the expense of the defensive will exceed that of the offensive." But the French advantage would disappear by the time of the Seven Years War and the coming of Lord William Pitt as Prime Minister of England. Determined to crush the French regime in Canada, Pitt would concentrate his forces in North America. The struggle for the continent would no longer be a sideshow.

OPPOSITE PAGE: *France's ships-of-the-line had three decks and were armed with 60 to 90 guns.* (LIBRARY OF PARLIAMENT)

🦢 DUC D'ANVILLE'S LUCKLESS FLEET

In 1746 the largest French fleet ever to cross the Atlantic comes to grief without firing a shot.

DETERMINED TO RECAPTURE Louisbourg, France sent out the largest fleet ever to cross the Atlantic in the spring of 1746. Commanded by the Duc d'Anville, a charming but inept nobleman with little experience at sea, the fleet was made up of 11 ships-of-the-line, 20 frigates, and 35 transports carrying 10,000 men.

Becalmed for a month at Île d'Aix, the fleet weighed anchor and finally set sail on June 22. It took over a month to reach the Azores and here another ten days were spent riding at anchor waiting for a suitable wind. When the winds came, they came in gale force, scattering the fleet. Several ships foundered and others returned to France. Typhus broke out and hundreds died. Finally, after three harrowing months at sea, the survivors struggled into Chebucto Bay, the future site of Halifax. The flagship *Northumberland* was brought safely in by a captured American pilot whose help had been secured with the threat of tying a couple of cannon balls to his feet and tossing him overboard.

At Chebucto, d'Anville had hoped to rendezvous with a squadron from the West Indies and several hundred troops from Quebec. While waiting on his forecastle deck, he died of an apoplectic fit, never learning that they had come and gone. His stricken crews were brought ashore to makeshift shelters beside the inner harbour where hundreds more died of cholera. Unaware of the danger, Micmac Indians took the clothes of the dead Frenchmen and spread the disease among their own people.

Command fell to Rear Admiral d'Estorelle who promptly tried to kill himself by falling on his sword. A new commander, the Marquis de la Jonquière, a future governor of New France, tried to salvage what he could out of the expedition. Hoping to take Port Royal, he mustered those still capable of handling sails and guns, and set out on October 22. Enveloped in thick fog, he abandoned the attack and set course for France.

The return journey was as bad as the voyage out. There were more storms, rations ran low, and even the sick had to be used to haul sail. Finally, on December 11, Jonquière limped into Port Louis at the end of the most disastrous expedition ever undertaken by the French navy: thousands dead without a shot ever having been fired.

In May of the following year, Jonquière sailed again with six fighting ships and a convoy of merchantmen only to be intercepted off Spain's Cape Finisterre by Admiral Anson. After a five-hour fight in which his flagship *Le Sérieux* took on ten feet of water in its hold and refused to answer its helm, he struck his colours. With Jonquière's surrender, the French fleet had virtually ceased to be.

OPPOSITE PAGE: *Founder of Halifax in 1749, Colonel Edward Cornwallis became Governor of Nova Scotia and later of Gibraltar. (PAC/c11070)*

THE FOUNDING OF HALIFAX

Named after the Lord of Trade and Plantations, the new settlement did well by its founding father, but the original inhabitants were another matter.

EVEN AS ENGLAND RETURNED Louisbourg to France, it took measures to neutralize it. On June 21, 1749, Lieutenant Colonel Edward Cornwallis sailed into Chebucto harbour with a dozen ships and 2000 settlers, charged with building a naval base and fortress.

At 36, Cornwallis was a well-connected career officer who had fought the French at Fontenoy and had participated in the slaughter of the Highland Scots at Culloden. Tall, slender and thoroughly aristocratic, he was unusual among contemporary governors in that he was incorruptible. If the new colony did well by its founding father, it could have done much better with its original inhabitants. "The ragtag and bobtail of London straight out of Hogarth's prints," one critic concluded. Although many were war veterans, lured by the promise of land and a year's supply of

Moses Haus, an 18-year-old entomologist and engraver, created this plan of the harbour of Chebucto and town of Halifax (with porcupine and butterflies) when he arrived with Cornwallis and his soldiers in 1749. (NOVA SCOTIA MUSEUM)

rations, once released from military discipline they degenerated into a mob of loafers, thieves and drunks. Most wanted only a chance to get to the New World, live on the King's rations and then hurry along to New England.

They stayed on the ships at first, but Cornwallis immediately ordered the men to start cutting trees along the waterfront. Within a month, they had cleared five hectares. Colonel Thomas Hopson, who had handed Louisbourg over to the French, arrived with the garrison from the fortress in August. Soon, he and his men were put to work building fortifications. Ships from Boston brought lumber and shingles, and huts, houses and streets began taking shape. During the day, the little settlement – named after the Earl of Halifax, Lord of Trade and Plantations – bustled with men and women going about their tasks. Night was given over to drunken revelries for there were makeshift taverns everywhere and rum was the staple beverage.

Cramped, dirty and subsisting on salt meat and hardtack, hundreds of the first Haligonians died of typhus in the winter of 1749-50. But as fast as the British died or fled, New Englanders took their place and the building went on. The Yanks were not universally popular. One settler wrote of them: "Of all the people upon earth I never heard any bear so bad a character for Cheating designing people & All under Ye Cloak of religion." They were joined by more than 2000 Germans, German-speaking Swiss and French Protestants recruited from southwestern Germany and the Montbéliard district on the border between France and Switzerland in an attempt to counter the French and Catholic presence in Nova Scotia. Some moved on to found a settlement at Lunenburg, Nova Scotia.

On September 11, 1749, Cornwallis reported to the Board of Trade that "the troops have been employed in carrying the Line of Palisades round the town according to the Plan sent our Lordships. The Square at the top of the Hill is finished. These squares are done with double picquets, each picquet ten foot long and six inches thick. They likewise clear a Space of 30 ft. without the Line and throw up the Trees by way of Barricade. When this Work is compleated I shall think the Town as secure against Indians as if it was regularly fortify'd."

To man the defences, Cornwallis had, in addition to the troops he brought with him, the regiments from Louisbourg and a company of Rangers commanded by John Gorham who had been brought over from Annapolis Royal. He needed these troops not only because of the obvious hostility of the Micmacs who were being incited to attack the settlement by the French, but also to maintain order among his own unruly settlers who were "inconceivably turbulent." After a raid in which four settlers were killed, he offered a reward of ten guineas for each Micmac, dead or alive. A "merry trade" ensued: French bought scalps at Louisbourg and the English at Halifax.

Broken in health, Cornwallis resigned as governor in 1752 to be succeeded by Hopson. His successor, Charles Lawrence, a tough, battle-scarred veteran, would secure the future of the colony and earn the hatred of generations of Acadians.

Halifax in the 1770s. No longer closed in by log palisades. The Union Jack flies from the Citadel, top left.
(PUBLIC ARCHIVES OF CANADA)

🐌 THE EXPULSION OF THE ACADIANS

Wanting nothing more than to be left in peace, the Acadians chose neutrality. In 1755 it would cost them their home.

"IF THAT ESTABLISHMENT succeeds we can give up Acadia," François Bigot, Intendant of New France, said of Halifax. And in the bitter autumn of 1755 his prophecy came true.

The French were always reluctant to yield Acadia, the site of their first colonial enterprise in North America. But under the terms of the Treaty of Utrecht, the colony passed into English hands and the inhabitants became subjects of the Crown. Passionately attached to their farms and villages around the Minas Basin and Annapolis, much of the land retrieved from the sea by a system of dikes, the Acadians wanted nothing more than to be left in peace. Offered the option of becoming British subjects or being moved to French territory, they chose neutrality, refusing to swear an oath of allegiance to the English king. That oath was expressed in simple terms: "I promise and sincerely swear by my Christian faith that I shall be entirely

RIGHT: *A monument at Grand-Pré celebrating the courage and tenacity of the Acadians.* (PARKS CANADA)

OPPOSITE PAGE: *This painting by Claude Picard depicts the sorrow of the Acadians as they are forced to leave their homes.*

faithful and shall truly obey His Majesty King George the Second whom I recognize as the Sovereign Lord of Acadia and Nova Scotia. So help me God."

During the years of peace between England and France, the matter of allegiance was not pressed too hard. Governors Cornwallis and Hopson exercised great patience with the Acadians, Hopson informing his officers that they were to be treated as if they were loyal subjects. "And if at any time the inhabitants should obstinately refuse to comply with what His Majesty's service may require of them," he wrote, "you are not to redress yourselves by military force or in an unlawful manner, but to lay the case before the Governor and wait his orders thereon." But with war clouds gathering, the Acadians came to be seen as a fifth column, enemy aliens within the borders of English territory. They seemed particularly threatening on the isthmus of Chignecto, a potential avenue for invading troops from Quebec.

The situation was inflamed by the Abbé Le Loutre, a scheming missionary described by Cornwallis as "a good for nothing Scoundrel as ever lived," who had organized Micmac raids on Halifax and who now used bribes and intimidation to induce the Acadians to take up arms. Many fought at Fort Beauséjour and were taken prisoner when the garrison surrendered to a force led by Colonel Robert Monckton. The articles of capitulation included the stipulation that "the Acadians, inasmuch as they were forced to take up arms under pain of death, shall be pardoned for the part they have taken." Governor Lawrence would have none of it, however, insisting that the Acadians immediately swear allegiance or be removed from their homes. When they refused, he issued orders to "get them out of the Country as soon as possible."

Down the Annapolis Valley, in the Cobequid country and along the rivers, British troops rounded up Acadians, herded them aboard transports. and burned their houses, barns and crops. At Grand Pré, Colonel John Winslow gathered the residents into the church while his soldiers guarded the doors and windows and informed them that "your lands and tenements and cattle and livestock of all kinds are forfeit to the Crown with all other effects, except money and household goods, and that you yourselves are to be removed from this province." In his journal, he wrote: "Began to embark the inhabitants who went off very unwillingly, the women in great distress carrying their children in their arms. Others carried their aged parents in their carts and all their goods moving in great confusion with woe and distress. The King's command was to me absolute and I did not love to use harsh means but that the time did not admit of parleys and delays, I ordered the troops to fix their bayonets and advance towards the French. This affair," he told a friend, "is more grievous to me than any service I was ever employed in."

Hundreds fled to Île St. Jean, trudged overland to Quebec, or hid in the woods where Charles Deschamps de Boishébert organized guerrilla warfare against the British. Joseph Brossard, the swashbuckling "Beausoleil," commanded a privateer manned by Acadians that captured British prizes in the Bay of Fundy. All to no avail as British settlers and New Englanders occupied their farms.

More than 6000 Acadians were deported and dispersed here and there along the Atlantic coast from Boston to Georgia. And in Louisiana, Longfellow's Évangeline would pine for Gabriel and her lost homeland.

OPPOSITE PAGE: *A young George Washington (mounted) leads the charge against the French.*

WAR IN THE WILDERNESS

Braddock marches to defeat on the Monongahela.

IN THE WEST, THE French seized the initiative. Acutely aware of the danger posed by American encroachment on lands they claimed by right of discovery, Governor La Galissonière proposed that a chain of forts be established in the Ohio Valley and that Indian tribes – the Delaware, Shawnee, and Seneca – be recruited as allies. In 1749, he dispatched an expedition led by Pierre Joseph de Céloron de Blainville to show the flag and forcibly remove settlers and traders. He then sent 2000 men to Lake Erie to construct a road to the headwaters of the Ohio River and build forts at strategic points. His successor, the only Canadian-born governor of New France, Pierre de Rigaud, Marquis de Vaudreuil, showed an equal awareness of the need for action and strengthened the garrisons in Illinois country.

All that the Americans could do to counter the erosion of their position was to send a young officer of the Virginia militia, Major George Washing-

ton, to the disputed territory with an escort of seven men and a letter from Governor Robert Dinwiddie demanding their immediate withdrawal. Jacques Le Gardeur, the grizzled commandant of Fort Le Boeuf, received Washington politely, but contemptuously dismissed Dinwiddie's ultimatum.

In 1754, a small force of Dinwiddie's militia attempted to establish a fort at the junction of the Ohio and Monongahela rivers (near present-day Pittsburgh). Work had just begun when a French force, 500 strong, swept down the upper Ohio River and forced them to beat a retreat across the Allegheny. The French then built Fort Duquesne on the site, dominating the entire region. Washington was dispatched once again, this time with a force of 300 men and orders to drive the French out.

Alarmed and edgy despite his experience with Indian warfare, Washington opened fire on a small party sent from Fort Duquesne to parley, killing ten, including the Sieur de Jumonville. Branded an "assassin" by the French, Washington in turn was attacked and forced to fall back on Great Meadows where he threw up a rough palisade which he called Fort Necessity. It was overlooked by a small ridge that allowed the French to riddle the place with musket fire. After a nine-hour battle in which he lost a third of his men, Washington ran up a white flag signed surprisingly generous capitulation terms, then hurriedly fled back to Virginia. In June, he was back as the second-in-command to Major General Edward Braddock who lead a force of 2200 regulars and militia.

RIGHT: *George Washington (1732-1799). Forced to surrender to the French at Fort Necessity in 1754, he was second-in-command to Braddock on the Monongahela. Once again, he had the unhappy task of leading a beaten army home.* (PEABODY COLLECTION, MARYLAND COMMISSION ON ARTISTIC PROPERTIES OF THE MAYLAND STATE ARCHIVES)

OPPOSITE PAGE: *In 1755, General Edward Braddock was shot from his horse while on his way to attack Fort Duquesne. His second-in-command, 23-year-old George Washington, led a beaten army back to Great Meadows.* (WISCONSIN STATE HISTORICAL SOCIETY)

An irascible man, "and very Iroquois in disposition," Braddock was a spit-and-polish officer of the Goldstream Guards, contemptuous of the colonial militia and totally unfamiliar with warfare in the wilderness, "I have a hundred and ten Miles to march thro' an uninhabited Wilderness over steep rocky Mountains and almost impassable Morasses," he wrote before setting off, That march was almost too much for him. He was forced to abandon most of his artillery, wagons broke down and the gloomy forest and tales of Indian ferocity sapped the morale of his men, The heat blistered faces and insects made life a torment to men who were new to the frontier. In late June he reached the ruins of Washington's Fort Necessity, and a few days later closed on Fort Duquesne.

In desperation, Captain Daniel de Beaujeu led a small force comprised of Compagnies Franches de la Marine, Canadian militia, and Indians out of the fort to oppose him. The clash was a disaster for the British. Taking cover behind trees, de Beaujeu's men raked the long lines of regulars with deadly flanking fire. Bayonets fixed, they moved forward in dressed ranks as if on parade, presenting irresistible targets in their red tunics, and webbing pipeclayed to a shining white. British volleys had little effect against the concealed enemy. When the French realized that, they fired on command to measured drumbeats, and began to pick off drummers and officers. Braddock was shot through the lungs. Confusion, then panic, spread through the British ranks. The troops broke and ran leaving behind 500 dead. The French lost 23 men.

Washington had the unhappy task of leading a beaten army home. At Great Meadows, the mortally wounded Braddock died after muttering, "Who could have thought it?" and a little later, "We shall better know how to deal with them another time."

❧ CLOSING THE RING

Self-assured, the French reinforce Quebec and seize Oswego as Wolfe sets sail for Louisbourg.

WITH BRADDOCK'S IGNOMINIOUS defeat, the French position in North America seemed assured. In the west, they were securely in possession of the Ohio Valley countryside from its upper reaches to the Mississippi River. From the nearer forts, war parties could fall on the rear of the English colonies at any time. In the east, Louisbourg was restored and to the south, strong garrisons at Forts Saint-Frédéric and Ticonderoga blocked the traditional invasion route into Canada. Ticonderoga also served as an advance base to attack Albany and the American frontier settlements, thereby containing sizable enemy forces. If necessary, the extended defence lines could be pulled back to Niagara and Fort Frontenac, lengthening American supply lines and making them more vulnerable to attack by French irregulars and their Indian allies.

Oswego on Lake Ontario posed a threat, but in July 1756 a force of

French regulars captured the fort after a four-day siege, taking 1700 British and American prisoners and a vast store of boats, cannons, small arms and ammunition. This was a stunning blow as it opened up the northwest frontier of New York to invasion. The entire frontier of the English colonies was now being ravaged by French and Indian war parties. Confidence that New France could be quickly conquered was replaced by fear that the French would soon invade the English colonies in force.

Only in the Maritimes did the French suffer a setback, with the loss of Fort Beauséjour and the expulsion of the Acadians. Those who made their way to Quebec served as a warning of what they could expect if they were defeated, inspiring them to fight with renewed ferocity.

At Quebec, the garrison was strengthened by the arrival of troops from France including the regiments of Béarn, La Reine, Guyenne, and Languedoc. Under the able command of Montcalm, Lévis, Louis-Antoine de Bougainville, and François-Charles de Bourlamaque, they would surely repulse any attempt to take the city. At the very least, the heart of New France would hold until hostilities ceased, leaving the mother country with a stronger position when the usual bargaining began at the peace table.

But these were unusual times. William Pitt was Prime Minister and Britannia ruled the waves. And in the Great Pontiac Hotel in Halifax a small group of British officers gathered for a banquet on the eve of sailing for Louisbourg. They consumed 25 bottles of brandy, 50 of claret, and 70 of Madeira. Their host was a young brigadier: James Wolfe.

🐚 HEARTS OF OAK

Disreputable, maltreated and mutinous,
British sailors win command of the seas.

FOUL-MOUTHED, drunken and dissolute, the 18th-century British sailor was hardly the Jolly Jack Tar of popular sea shanties. Press-ganged into service, ill-paid, ill-fed, and ill-cared for, his life was nasty, brutal and often short. Nor was he the neatly-turned out seafarer of picture books. Few captains insisted that uniforms be worn. As a result, ship's companies looked like a band of ragged and shabby pirates. After long years of service, if he survived, a sailor could count on nothing more than to be discharged into an old age of beggary.

Mortality in the fleet was terrible. There was no medical examination of recruits, few of the principles of sanitation were known and those few seldom observed. Naval hospitals, whether afloat or ashore, were totally inadequate. Of the 184,893 sailors and marines that served during the Seven Years War, 1512 were killed in action and 133,708 died of sickness or were listed as missing.

OPPOSITE PAGE: *In the 18th century, men did not generally volunteer easily for service. In this drawing, a lieutenant with a party of seamen are impressing men for service in the Royal Navy at Tower Hill, London. (NATIONAL MARITIME MUSEUM)*

The "missing" were mostly deserters. Most hated their lot and escaped from it at the first opportunity. As a consequence, discipline was brutal. It was not particularly strict, as sailors were allowed a wide leeway that would not be tolerated now, but when a rule was broken, punishment was severe. The sailor and the cat-o'-nine-tails were on intimate terms. Yet, these men, disreputable, maltreated and mutinous, fought splendidly, winning command of the seas. That command was not assured. The French excelled at naval construction with British captains always delighted to get the command of a French prize. Timber, tackle, rigging and guns were also superior. But in the end, numbers and better seamanship would prevail.

At the beginning of the Seven Years War, Britain had 72 ships-of-the-line, France 34. Still, numbers are not everything and the quality of French ships might well have told more had it not been for the inferiority of the crews. The sea-faring population of Britain was much greater in proportion to the number of ships she sailed than was that of France. No matter what losses the British suffered, there were always suitable reserves. But as the war went on, France had to replace many of her lost sailors with landsmen – and the French navy did not attract the best officers. It was treated as a subsidiary to the army and it was the army that offered the most alluring opportunities to young noblemen. By contrast, in Britain the navy was the Senior Service, the people were proud of it and the army was still regarded with lingering suspicion, dating from Cromwell's day as a potential instrument of tyranny. There was no shortage of young men of real promise eager to serve, drawn from families with a tradition of naval service going back generations. The British quarterdeck knew its job and did it.

Nor was a British captain likely to forget that his first duty was to destroy the enemy. When Edward Boscawen was awakened one night with the news that two French men-of-war were bearing down on his ship he was asked by an ensign, "What's to be done?"

"Why, damn it, fight 'em!" he replied as he rolled out of his bunk. It was that spirit that would chase the French from the seas, land Jeffrey Amherst safely at Louisbourg, and James Wolfe at Quebec.

BELOW: *A popular cartoon depicting an imaginary scene aboard HMS* Téméraire *at Trafalgar.*

OPPOSITE PAGE: *A capable commander and a savage critic of most of his colleagues, the Marquis de Montcalm (1712-1759) spent four campaigning seasons trying to make the defence of New France conform to European styles of warfare. His greatest battle would take place in 1759 at the Plains of Abraham.* (PAC/C27665)

A EUROPEAN SENSIBILITY

*A savage critic of most of his colleagues,
Montcalm tried to make the defence of
New France conform to European styles of
warfare.*

IT MAY BE SIMPLISTIC to say that Britain intended to win the war against France in Canada while France intended to defend Canada by winning the war in Europe. Other interests were involved. France had recently formed an alliance with her old enemy, Austria, while Britain had taken up with Prussia; and the Austrians and Prussians didn't care a damn about Canada. But William Pitt, the British prime minister who masterminded his country's prosecution of the Seven Years War, saw victory in Canada as the key to Britain's future greatness. Under Pitt, the war in Canada would no longer be about fur; it would be about territory. It would also be a settling of scores dating back to Champlain's time.

From the outbreak of war in 1756, the war in Canada was to be war European style, fought by regular armies and directed towards the end of a decisive close-order battle. Although the French and their Indian allies would continue to wage *la petite guerre* in the forests with ambushes, scalping raids, and extemporized sieges, the strategic balance now depended on who could bring the largest conventional forces to bear at the key point – Quebec.

France sent strong reinforcements to Quebec in the spring of 1756, including the white coat regular regiments of La Salle, Berry, and Roussillon, under the command of a competent general, Louis-Joseph, Marquis de Montcalm-Gozon de Saint-Veran. Montcalm was 47, a minor noble from Languedoc in a nation overrun with petty nobility. He began his military service as a boy and served with distinction in Italy and Bohemia during the War of the Austrian Succession (1740-48). Always at the front, he was wounded three times. Promoted to *maréchal de camp* (major general), he was sent to Canada with orders from the king to place himself under the authority of Governor General Pierre de Rigaud de Vaudreuil in all matters except the discipline and disposition of the regular *troupes de terre*. Short, quick-tempered, determined, and vain, Montcalm was Vaudreuil's physical and temperamental opposite.

Lord Loudoun, the British commander-in-chief in North America, also brought reinforcements: the 35th and 42nd Foot (the Black Watch), the 50th and 51st as well as a contingent of Royal Artillery. He had orders to raise a regular regiment in the colonies — to be numbered the 60th (Royal Americans) — and to strengthen the provincial corps of militia. With powerful field and siege artillery, he was supported offshore by a fleet of 15 ships-of-the-line and 23 smaller vessels. Although he was an able administrator with a passion for paperwork, Loudoun showed little inclination for engaging the enemy. One American remarked that the general "was like St. George upon the signposts, always on horseback but never advancing."

Accompanied by his aide-de-camp, Louis-Antoine de Bougainville, a noted mathematician and one of the few men to be elected to both the Royal Society and the Académie des Sciences, Brigadier François-Gaston, Duc de Lévis, his second-in-command and a man of humble origins who had proved himself a superb soldier, and François-Charles de Bourlamaque, his chief engineer, Montcalm arrived in Quebec on May 12, 1756 to a restrained welcome.

Montcalm and Vaudreuil despised each other and were soon writing regularly to France informing their superiors of the other's shortcomings. "Monsieur Montcalm has got so quick a temper," Vaudreuil wrote to the Minister of Marine "that he goes as far as to strike the Canadians." Vaudreuil, in turn, was described as "a timid man and one who neither knows how to make a resolution or to keep one once made." Nor was Montcalm sparing of Vaudreuil's subordinates, complaining to Lévis that "Mercier is a weakling and an ignoramus, Saint-Luc a garrulous braggart, Montigny admirable, but a looter, Marin brave, but stupid, the rest are not worth mentioning."

The first Canadian-born governor, Vaudreuil sneered at Montcalm and his staff as foppish parade-ground soldiers who knew nothing about campaigning in Canada. Through guerrilla tactics and shrewd deployment of his limited military resources, Vaudreuil had been able to thwart the larger British forces and American militia. He was full of confidence, dispatching flotillas of canoes and bateaux to reinforce the garrisons at Niagara, Frontenac, Crown Point, and Ticonderoga. Impressed by his victories and enticed by French promises of scalps and plunder, the Mohawk, Abenaki, Ottawa, Ojibwa, Potawatomi, Sauk, and Fox from the *pays d'en haut* rallied to Vaudreuil's cause.

Montcalm hated these tactics and the governor's Indian allies. "It is no longer the time," he said, "when a few scalps, or the burning of a few houses is any advantage or even an object. Petty means, petty ideas, petty councils about details are now dangerous."

In the first battles of the war, Montcalm took Fort Oswego on the south shore of Lake Ontario using traditional tactics — siege guns and French regulars — while the Canadians and Indians raided outposts on the Mohawk River portages. Montcalm saw the alliance with the Indians as a necessary evil, concerned that his troops would abandon the conventions of European warfare and embrace the savagery of the new landscape. "They make war with astounding cruelty," he wrote of the Indians. "They are *villains messieurs*, sparing neither men, women or children, and take off your scalp very neatly — in an operation which generally kills you."

Bougainville, whose wit, erudition and withering comments about provincial Canadians delighted Montcalm, immersed himself in Indian culture, though he too held on to his European sensibilities. "Their souls are

LEFT: *Pierre de Rigaud de Vaudreuil, the son of the governor who had led New France early in the 18th century, himself became governor general in 1755. A Canadian by birth, Vaudreuil knew the importance of maintaining alliances with the native peoples and the use of frontier raids in fighting the British, both contrary to Montcalm's beliefs.* (PUBLIC ARCHIVES OF CANADA)

OPPOSITE PAGE: *Contrary to Montcalm's prejudices, the Hurons were a complex and well-organized people, with a distinct civilization and culture, living in large and established communities.* (NATIONAL ARCHIVES OF CANADA)

as black as pitch," he noted in his journal. "It is an abominable way to wage war; the retaliation is frightening, and the air one breathes here is contagious of making one accustomed to callousness... This country is dangerous for discipline. Pray God that it alone suffers from it."

Nevertheless, he and Montcalm embarked on a goodwill tour of Indian villages "to sing the war song" and recruit warriors for a planned assault on Fort William Henry. "In the midst of the woods of America," Montcalm wrote, "one can no more do without them than without cavalry in open country."

At Sault St. Louis, Bougainville attended a council with the Nipissing, Algonquin, and Iroquois at which each chief stood up and sang a war song. When implored to do the same, he adopted the listing cadence of the music and repeated the phrase "Trample the English underfoot" until he was exhausted. The next night he was adopted by the Iroquois in a tribal ceremony and given the name *Garionatsigoa*, meaning "Great Angry Sky." "Behold me then," the diminutive, overweight, and asthmatic Bougainville wrote in his journal, "an Iroquois war chief!"

Fort William Henry was new, a strengthened version of the camp which William Johnson, the Indian superintendent of New York, had pitched at the bottom of Lac St. Sacrement (now Lake George), the southern arm of Lake Champlain, in 1745. It was not the only fort built during the muscle-

flexing days leading up to war in which both sides tried to match their antagonist fortress for fortress. Farther up Lake Champlain, the French restored Fort Saint Frédéric at Crown Point and built Fort Carillon on the tinkling falls at Ticonderoga, where the two lakes joined. The British followed suit with Forts Edward, Bull, Williams, and William Henry.

By the standards of North American military construction, Fort William Henry was a formidable presence. Flanked by marshes, protected by a log stockade, a palisaded outpost and gravel embankments, it mounted seventeen cannon, mortars and swivel guns to guard the wilderness trail leading to Fort Edward. The surrounding slopes, down to the water's edge, had been burned over to deny an approaching enemy cover. Lt.-Col. George Munro, the fort's commanding officer, "an old officer, but one who had never served in the field," could muster more than 1,500 men. It did, however, have two serious flaws: it lacked outer works that might prevent an enemy from entrenching close enough to launch an artillery bombardment and it was too small.

Montcalm led his force out of Carillon on July 30 and embarked in a fleet of boats and canoes. He had 3,600 regulars and militiamen, 1,500 Indians, and a dozen cannon. He was also soon in possession of a letter to Munro from nearby Fort Edward warning that no help could be expected. Montcalm proceeded to make a proper show of force, setting up batteries and digging saps forward in the best European siege style. The effect was so impressive that it took only three days of bombardment to persuade Munro to accept defeat. He and his garrison marched out to captivity in a display of military courtesy. Then, the trouble began.

The terms of surrender, so honourable by European conventions of war, were completely alien to Montcalm's Indian allies. Moreover, they had been negotiated without consulting them, with total disregard for what they considered to be their legitimate expectations. They had fought bravely and the only rewards they asked for were plunder, trophies to prove their prowess in battle, and captives to adopt or ransom. When it became clear that Montcalm would deny them, most of the warriors decided merely to take what they had come for and then leave. And that is exactly what they did.

As the garrison marched out, the Indians swooped into the fort in search of booty and, finding little, set upon the sick and wounded who had been left to be cared for by the French. Other warriors harassed the terrified prisoners, taunting them and stealing their personal goods.

Montcalm let it be known that he planned to march the prisoners to Fort Edward in the morning. This was a deception, as he hoped to spirit them away during the night before the Indians realized what was happening. It was an ill-conceived plan that only further antagonized the Indians who were now convinced that the French and English were in league to deny them their spoils. When the long column of prisoners finally moved out, it was beset on every side.

"The Marquis de Montcalm rushed up at the noise," Bougainville wrote, "several French officers risked their lives in tearing the English from the hands of the Indians. Finally, the disorder quieted down and he at once took away from the Indians four hundred of these unfortunate men and had them clothed. The French officers divided with the English officers the few spare clothes they had."

By the time order could be restored, as many as 185 soldiers and camp followers had been killed and a much larger number — between 300 and 500 — had been taken captive. The Indians left without delay on the long journey home once they had secured the prisoners, scalps and plunder they claimed were rightfully theirs — earned in battle.

Montcalm and Vaudreuil did their best to intercept warriors returning to the *pays d'en haut* in order to ransom their captives. At least 200 prisoners were recovered by the end of August, at an average cost to the Crown of 130 livres and thirty bottles of brandy each. Vaudreuil hoped to minimize the damage to French-Indian relations from an incident the Indians regarded as a betrayal of trust and one which Montcalm, with equal conviction, saw as sheer savagery. Thus, he did his best to appease both the commander-in-chief (by ransoming as many prisoners as possible) and the Indians (by offering the most generous terms he could afford). All to no avail.

Never again would the Indians flock to the French colours as they had in 1757. The western tribes would discover too late that the English at Fort William Henry had been suffering from smallpox, and that the captives, scalps, and clothing they brought back carried the seeds of a great epidemic that would devastate their homelands. No warrior from the *pays d'en haut* would ever help Montcalm again. He would have to rely on regulars and Canadians to oppose the regulars and provincials of the British, fighting more and more in the European style he preferred.

But British officers would be disinclined to offer European honours of war to any French force. And British outrage over the massacre at Fort William Henry would intensify an undiscriminating hatred of Indians.

French cannoniers-bombardiers manoeuvering an artillery piece into place.
(RECONSTITUTION BY EUGENE LELIEPVRE, CANADIAN PARKS SERVICE)

ᔐ BATTLE OF CARILLON

"What a day for France! What soldiers are ours!" Montcalm marvelled as he raised a great cross to celebrate a victory "wrought by God."

WHILE THE FALL OF Fort William Henry marked a critical juncture in the war, its long-term significance took some time to understand. The British saw it as one more humiliation; one more instance of military incompetence in the dismal litany of defeat the war had become.

After Montcalm's victory, nothing seemed to prevent him from taking the next logical objective: Fort Edward. Instead, he opted to destroy Fort William Henry and return to Fort Carillon. The British were greatly relieved without understanding why. Montcalm, however, had had no choice but to withdraw, for he was hobbled by the loss of his Indian allies and an acute shortage of provisions.

New France had suffered a disastrous crop failure in 1756 and Montcalm was compelled to release the Canadian militiamen who made up more than

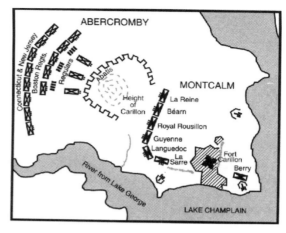

RIGHT: *Map showing the assault on Fort Carillon, July 1758. (BY THOMAS CONLEY)*

OPPOSITE PAGE: *Montcalm prepares the Languedoc Regiment for battle. (ILLUSTRATION BY JAMES C. TILLY, NAC/c-020695)*

half of his force, for they were urgently needed to return home for the harvest. Even this did not prevent further disaster, for the harvest of 1757 would be one of the worst in Canadian history. Conditions were particularly bad around Montreal, "the granary of Canada." By late September, the inhabitants were subsisting on a half-pound of bread a day, and those at Quebec on half that. A month later, there was no bread at all. "The distress is so great that some of the inhabitants are living on grass," Bougainville wrote. There was a feeling of abject despair in the colony and no one contemplating its military prospects could escape the conclusion that it would soon become indefensible.

The second event that accompanied the fall of Fort William Henry was equally significant: the mobilization of thousands of New England militiamen. While Canada would grow weaker and more difficult to defend, the colonies had demonstrated a capacity to respond to a military emergency without parallel in the English-speaking world. If only some means could be found to effectively direct them, the energies and manpower of the northern colonies alone could tip the strategic balance in North America. Yet, when the British took to the offensive the following year, not much seemed to have changed. The first blow to be struck brought only defeat. With the possible exception of Braddock's defeat on the Monongahela, Montcalm's victory over General James Abercrombie at Fort Carillon on July 8, 1758, would result in Britain's greatest humiliation of the war.

Montcalm's strategy was to hold the enemy at bay until reinforcements arrived from France – an unlikely proposition given that Louis XV was not inclined to send more soldiers to defend what Voltaire called a "few acres of snow" – or until French victories elsewhere in the world forced the British to seek a negotiated peace. France might then save Canada by swapping other conquests for its losses in North America. To that end, Montcalm decided to concentrate his forces at Carillon, the southernmost French outpost, anticipating they would eventually fall back to Quebec and Montreal.

Vaudreuil, and many others, accused the general of being a defeatist, pointing out that for more than a century Canadians had resisted the British and had often carried out successful raids deep into enemy territory. Vaudreuil argued that small forces moving aggressively against the British would force them to disperse their army. "It is in the true and fundamental interest of the colony that I devote my main efforts to defending the soil of our frontiers foot by foot against the enemy," he wrote to the minister of war, "whereas M. de Montcalm and the 'troupes de la terre' seek only to preserve their reputation and would like to return to France without having suffered a single defeat."

The British commanders had a problem of a different sort – they had to operate under the unblinking eye of Prime Minister William Pitt, who was determined to manage every aspect of the campaign. His secretaries could hardly keep up with him. On December 30, 1757, he sent no fewer than nine separate dispatches to America. These included Lord Loudoun's recall, Abercrombie's appointment, instructions to governors, and detailed plans for the campaign in 1758. Abercrombie was to concentrate on Carillon and Crown Point, Jeffrey Amherst was to take Louisbourg, and John Forbes was to march on Fort Duquesne. Although Abercrombie, like Braddock and Loudoun before him, bore the title "Commander in Chief of His Majesty's Forces in North America," thanks to Pitt's interference he really commanded only the forces with him in person, moving against Carillon. By early summer, as militia regiments arrived from Massachusetts, New Hampshire, New York, Connecticut, Rhode Island, and New Jersey, these numbered nearly twenty thousand. But they were ill-disciplined and ill-trained.

Captain Hugh Arnot of the 18th Regiment spat out his opinion: "The greater their Numbers, the greater the Evil; for of any set of people in the

Universe they are the worst cut out for war. The most stupid and most chicken-hearted set of Mankind." Abercrombie had only a few days to drill them before they marched off to the assembly point at Lake George.

Abercrombie, a Scot like Loudoun, was a seasoned soldier, but he had never before held a major independent command. Described by his contemporaries as "heavy," "aged" (he was 52), and "infirm in mind and body," he had more political clout than military ability. As his friend Loudoun delicately put it: "Abercrombie is a good officer and a very good second Man anywhere, whatever he is employed in." Fortunately, he had a very good second man, Lord George Howe, "the very Spirit and Life of the Army."

Lord George Augustus, Third Viscount Howe, the 34-year-old brother of Richard and William who would win fame in the American Revolution, was unusual among British officers, with all the vigour, youth, and dash that Abercrombie lacked. Everyone loved Lord Howe, from senior officers to illiterate privates, from Pitt who praised him as "a complete model of military virtue" to Howe's American hostess, Mrs. Schuyler, who actually wept when he went off to battle.

Howe had taken the time to study wilderness warfare with Major Robert Rogers and his Rangers – living as they lived, relying on the land for food, water, and shelter. At Rogers's suggestion, Howe ordered his men to throw away their lace cuffs, cut their hair short, wear leather leggings as protection in the forests, and to travel light. Howe also taught the men new techniques in fire and movement, including shooting and reloading from covered positions. One of his officers commented: "Regulars as well as Provincials cut their coats so as scarcely to reach their waists. No officer or private is allowed to carry more than one blanket and a bearskin." And, most telling of all, he added: "No women followed the camp to wash our linen. Lord Howe has already set an example by going to the brook and washing his own."

On July 5, as drummers beat "The General," the call to fall in, the regiments marched towards the boats assembled along the south shore of Lake George. First off were Lieutenant Colonel John Bradstreet's bateauxmen, who formed a skirmish line ahead of the light infantry on the right and the Rangers on the left. The main body came next, with artillery barges, commissary stores, and hospital boats closing up the rear. More than a thousand small craft "covered the Lake from side to side" in lines that "extended from Front to Rear full seven Miles."

Located on a peninsula between Lake George and Lake Champlain, Fort Carillon, which the British called Ticonderoga, was a small fort with serious disadvantages. Within its walls there was barely space for a single battalion, while outside the fort the terrain to the west, particularly Rattlesnake Mountain, was high enough to allow an enemy to range artillery. Bourlamaque, Montcalm's chief engineer, said that if he were the attacking general he "would require only six mortar and two cannon for its complete reduction." Carillon would have to be defended by holding the ground outside the walls.

Montcalm's force consisted of eight battalions of French regulars, numbering approximately 3000 men, 400 militia of the Compagnies Franches de la Marine, and a few Indians. The garrison had only enough food to last for nine days and an emergency ration of 3600 biscuits. Bourlamaque, in command until Montcalm arrived, had already sent a courier to Vaudreuil begging for more provisions. None were forthcoming. "Our situation is critical," Bougainville wrote. "Action and audacity are our sole resources."

At daybreak, on July 6, Abercrombie and his men were within sight of the French advance guard, a camp at the foot of Lake George just four miles from Fort Carillon. The French troops fled, abandoning "a considerable amount of valuable baggage which our men plundered," wrote Rufus Putman, a Massachusetts militiamen. Lord Howe, with the Rangers and light infantry, set off through dense bush in pursuit of the retreating enemy. Before anyone quite knew what had happened he was dead, killed by a musket ball in a confused skirmish at Bernetz Brook. Captain Alexander Monypenny, Howe's brigade major, described the action:

"When the firing began on the left part of the column, Lord Howe, thinking it would be of the greatest consequence to beat the enemy with the light troops, so as not to stop the march of the main body, went up with them, and had just gained the top of a hill, where the firing was, when he was killed. Never ball had more deadly direction. It entered his breast on the left side, and (as the surgeons say) pierced his lungs and heart, and shattered his backbone. I was six yards from him, he fell on his back and never moved, only his hands quivered an instant."

Howe had trained his men well and they pressed forward, killing, wounding, or capturing nearly half the French force, setting an example that the rest of the army found difficult to follow. News of the general's death, and fear of the Indians, "threw our Regulars in to some kind of Consternation," wrote Major William Eyre. Indeed, consternation and confusion became the order of the day as Abercrombie and his officers struggled to regain control of the army. Frightened troops, with reckless disregard for standing orders, fired blindly into the woods, killing a number of their comrades. As darkness fell, the entire army was back where it had started the day – on the shore of the lake.

The action at Bernetz Brook had bought time for Montcalm and he used it well. To avoid envelopment he withdrew his force closer to Carillon and by dusk all the French regiments were assembled on the heights between the fort and the anticipated British line of advance. Work gangs cleared and staked out fields of fire, while each regiment was assigned a 100-yard sector along a defensive line of trenches that were protected by a log breastwork topped with sandbags. The line zigzagged across the top of the ridge in such a way that the whole front could be swept by flanking fire. Officers and men worked together in the July heat, digging and felling trees on the slope to the west of the fort to build an elaborate abatis – a tangled mass of sharpened and interlaced branches and tree trunks. Like modern concertina wire, this provided a highly effective barrier against infantry. A Massachusetts officer later wrote that it looked like "a forest laid flat by a hurricane."

Artillery was always the key to siege warfare, and here, with sixteen cannon, eleven mortars, and thirteen howitzers, lay Abercrombie's greatest advantage. If he had secured Rattlesnake Mountain (later named Mount Defiance), which rose about 700 feet above the lake a little over a mile to the southwest of Carillon, and hauled two or three twelve-pounders to its summit he would have been able to fire into Montcalm's rear, forcing him to withdraw. At the very least, he could have advanced his howitzers to the edge of the clearing to smash the breastworks before launching an assault.

As it happened, Abercrombie dispatched a very junior lieutenant to survey the French lines on the morning of July 8. After a hasty inspection, he advised the general that Carillon could be carried by storm. Abercrombie

LEFT: *The losing commander of the British-American army at Ticonderoga in 1758, General James Abercromby was referred to by his aboriginal allies as the "Old Squah who should wear Petticoats."* (PAINTING BY ALLAN RAMSAY)

OPPOSITE PAGE: *This famous painting by Harry Ogden depicts Montcalm celebrating his victory at Carillon, with his soldiers.* (COURTESY DAVID M. STEWART MUSEUM)

did not bother to take a look himself or consult Major Eyre, his vastly experienced engineer. Nor did he order his artillery forward from the landing place, where it remained. Infantry alone would bear the burden of the battle. According to Eyre, Abercrombie told his staff: "We must Attack Any Way, and not be losing time in talking or consulting how."

A little after ten, skirmishers emerged from the tree line, driving in the French pickets and taking up sniping positions. Then 7000 regulars in bright scarlet formed ranks along battalion fronts and advanced in three long parallel lines straight up against the French barricade. The Black Watch, in the centre, marched off to the wail of bagpipes. As they came within range, the French opened fire with deadly effect, firing at a rate three to five times that of the British, as less skilled troops reloaded and passed muskets to the marksmen. Montcalm directed the defence with his coat off, moving to any part of the line where the danger seemed greatest. Volley after volley swept the British lines and cannons spewed great swaths of grapeshot.

All along the front, command and control on the British side collapsed as the heavily laden troops stumbled into the abatis and were cut down. Caught in a nightmare of branches, stumps, cannon fire, and musketry, none reached the French lines.

"Our orders were to run to the breastwork and get in if we could," a survivor recalled. "But their lines were full, and they killed our men so fast,

that we could not gain it. We got behind trees, logs and stumps, and covered ourselves as best we could from the enemy's fire. The ground was strewed with the dead and dying. It happened that I got behind a white-oak stump, which was so small that I had to lay on my side, and stretch myself; the balls striking the ground within a hand's breadth of me every moment, and I could hear the men screaming, and see them dying all around me."

No regiment suffered more than the Black Watch, which got to within twenty paces of the French line before being driven back with devastating losses; "cut down like grass," in the words of a witness. But the highlanders attacked again, "like roaring lions breaking from their chains." By seven in the evening, however, they and nearly all of the regulars who could still walk had retreated behind a line held by the provincials, leaving their dead and most of the wounded behind them.

Far to the rear, Abercrombie, ridiculed by his men and Indian allies as "Mrs. Nabbycrombie" and the "Old Squah who should wear Petticoats," had ordered attacks all day without seeing any of the consequences. Now, at nightfall, fearing a French counterattack, he began to comprehend what his army had suffered with nearly 2000 dead and wounded. "It was therefore judged necessary," he later reported to Pitt, "for the Preservation of the Remainder of so many brave Men, that we should make the best retreat possible." Unfortunately, he did not tell the men why they were retreating and panic set in. By dawn on July 9, the largest British army ever assembled in America was rowing for its life up Lake George, fleeing an enemy not a quarter its size – and not in pursuit.

Montcalm's army, which had lost 377 men, bivouacked for the night between their breastwork and the fort, fully expecting to resume the battle the following day. At first, Montcalm believed the retreat was a ruse, and waited for two days before sending out patrols "to find what had become of the enemy army." Only then, when they found hastily abandoned wounded, provisions, and piles of equipment, did he realize the extent of his victory. "The army, the too-small army of the King, has beaten the enemy!" he wrote triumphantly to his friend Doreil in Quebec. "What a day for France! If I had two hundred Indians to send out at the head of a thousand picked men under the Chevalier de Lévis, not many would have escaped. Ah my dear Doreil, what soldiers are ours! I never saw the like."

As Montcalm and his men sang a Te Deum of thanksgiving, even so hardheaded a rationalist as Bougainville said, "never had a victory been more especially due to the finger of Providence." The marquis himself was moved to compose a Latin couplet and have it inscribed on a great cross which he ordered erected at the breastwork:

Quid dux? Quid miles? Squid strata igentia ligna?
En signum! En victor! Deus hic, Deus ipse triumphat

To whom belongs this victory? Commander? Soldier? Abatis?
Behold God's sign! For only He Himself hath triumphed here

LEFT: "Like Roaring Lions breaking from their chains," so an eyewitness described the 42nd Foot, Royal Highlanders (later to become famous as The Black Watch), when they mounted a ferocious assault through the nearly impenetrable abatis in front of the French entrenchments on the heights of Carillon on July 8, 1758. The artist has erroneously placed Fort Carillon behind the French position when in fact it was a half mile down the hill and out of sight. (WATERCOLOUR BY C.C.P. LAWSON, COURTESY OF THE BLACK WATCH OF CANADA MUSEUM)

OPPOSITE PAGE: All of the events of September 13, 1759 are depicted in this engraving based on Wolfe's aide-de-camp Harvey Smith's drawing.

THE PLAINS OF ABRAHAM

On September 13, 1759, the future of New France lays in the balance as Wolfe and Montcalm face off on the Plains of Abraham.

WITHIN DAYS OF HIS VICTORY at Carillon, Montcalm dispatched Bougainville to Paris with the news. Yet, even in victory, the marquis remained ungenerous toward the Canadians. He disparaged their role in his triumph and condemned them for allegedly cowardly behaviour. Weeks later, as he contemplated the situation in Canada, he plunged into gloom. According to Montcalm, the "Grand Society" over which Intendant François Bigot presided, consumed all commerce. Canada was in dire straits: agriculture was faltering, the population was diminishing, and war was ever present. Bougainville summed it up well when he wrote to his wife: "Can we hope for another miracle to save us? I trust in God; he fought for us on the 8th of July."

But there would be no more miracles. Too strapped for men and provisions to take the offensive, Montcalm spent the rest of the summer improving Carillon's fortifications. Reconnaissance patrols sent to Lake George brought back news which indicated that Abercromby had also gone on the defensive. Yet, Montcalm knew that unless the war ended soon, some British general would return to try to take Carillon. It would be weeks before he heard more momentous news – the loss of Louisbourg and the destruction of Fort Frontenac. On the evening of September 6, as couriers brought word of these defeats, he left for Montreal to confer with Vaudreuil. The season was so far advanced that there was little chance that Canada would come under attack before the next spring. But news of these defeats and the suspicion that Vaudreuil was conspiring against him filled Montcalm with dreadful foreboding.

As well they might, military successes at Louisbourg and elsewhere consolidated Pitt's power as prime minister and he would henceforth not back away from his goal of taking Canada and stripping France of her empire, and he could see no sense whatsoever in Vaudreuil's plans for the defence of Canada.

Vaudreuil saw the problem of defence in light of the traditional strategies of Indian alliances and *la petite guerre*. This rested upon his confidence that, although the British might conquer territory, they could never hold it so long as the Canadians and their Indian allies remained united and capable of resisting in the interior. The true security of New France, he believed, lay in keeping open communication with the tribes of the *pays d'en haut*, for these warriors could visit such havoc on the enemy's frontiers that the British would eventually be forced to sue for peace. While his plans envisioned the defence of Quebec, his overall strategy called for a staged withdrawal westward, rather than a supreme effort to stop the enemy outside the walls of the city, and Quebec itself might be abandoned without crippling the colony's defences.

As a conventionally minded European soldier, Montcalm thought that Vaudreuil's plans were suicidal. In his view, the key to Canada was Quebec and the only way to hold it was to concentrate his forces there. Montcalm did not discount the value of Indian allies, but after his experience at Fort William Henry, he distrusted them as unreliable, uncontrollable, and barbarous. Nor did he wish to rely on the Canadians. The rapacity of Bigot and his cronies and their preference for irregular warfare had led him to disdain the military abilities of the people he had been sent to defend. He therefore intended to contract the perimeter of defence to the St. Lawrence Valley from Quebec to Montreal. If the British could be repulsed on the ramparts of Quebec, Canada might be preserved until a general peace was concluded in Europe, and the prewar frontiers might be restored diplomatically. If, on the other hand, the colony should fall, at least he would have the satisfaction of having conducted an honourable defence, and honour rather than victory meant everything to Montcalm.

Until Bougainville arrived back from France in May 1759, with new directives from King Louis XV – and much-needed supplies and reinforcements – Vaudreuil had conducted Canada's defence. Now, promoted to lieutenant-general, Montcalm was in charge and his strategic vision prevailed. Carillon, Crown Point, and Fort Duquesne on the Ohio – the key to the *pays d'en haut* – were abandoned and every available soldier was pulled back to the vicinity of Quebec. All the regulars in Canada except Bourlamaque's three battalions were there: Bearn, Guyenne, Languedoc, La Sarre, and the Royal-Roussillon. So too were the militia companies of New France, including old men and boys, sailors, Acadian refugees, some 800 Indians from the local missions, and 35 students from Quebec's Jesuit seminary – a unit so improbable that it was dubbed the Royal-Syntaxe. Montcalm integrated the best of the militiamen into the regulars (their ranks depleted after years of warfare), and set the rest to work fortifying the countryside around the city.

Quebec was a natural fortress, perched on a promontory rising 200 to 350 feet above the north shore of the St. Lawrence, at the point where the river narrows. The Upper Town was secure within its walls, looking down on the houses and docks of Lower Town and the suburbs of St-Roch and Palais. Below the city, the St. Charles River flowed into the St. Lawrence, flanked by a steep escarpment. Downriver, for about three miles, the banks of the St. Lawrence are relatively flat, until, at the village of Beauport, the land begins to rise for another three miles to the Montmorency River and its spectacular waterfall, which one of General James Wolfe's men would later describe as "a stupendous natural curiosity." Above Quebec, steep wooded slopes, bluffs, and cliffs lined the river's northern shore for miles.

Lieutenant-Colonel Cockburn often supervised drill at Quebec City and illustrated the practices. (PAC)

West of the city lay farmland that flattened into a narrow plateau between the St. Lawrence and St. Charles rivers, where apothecary Abraham Martin had settled to farm in the early 17th century. There, on what came to be known as the Plains of Abraham, level ground swept gently upward through farms and wood lots to a slight ridge, and then on to the walls of Quebec.

Montcalm evacuated Île-aux-Coudres and Île d'Orléans and positioned most of his men below the city in the Parish of Beauport, in a maze of trenches supported by artillery batteries, with the St. Lawrence in front of them, the St. Charles to their right, and the Montmorency to the left. The regulars held the centre of the line, with the militias of Quebec, Montreal, and Trois-Rivières on the flanks. Although the militias were of little use in the open field, Montcalm trusted them to fight well from fortified positions. Another fortified line, an extensive earthwork, was laid out north of the St. Charles, which was blocked by logs and armed hulks chained together at its mouth. Below the city, several of the recently arrived supply ships were fitted out as fire ships, which could be drifted downstream against the enemy. Meanwhile, their crews and seamen who had moved their ships up the St. Lawrence beyond the Richelieu were assigned to gunboats and a floating battery mounting twelve guns. Montcalm could muster more than 14,000 men in addition to the 2000-man garrison of the city under the command of Chevalier Jean-Baptiste-Nicolas-Roch de Ramezay.

When all was in readiness, Montcalm, Vaudreuil, and the city waited… and waited.

In the aftermath of the debacle at Fort Carillon, the hapless Abercromby had been replaced by Jeffrey Amherst, a well-connected young officer, barely 40 years old, who had made his name at Louisbourg along with Admiral

A general view of Quebec from across the St. Lawrence at Point Lévis in 1761. (PAINTING BY RICHARD SHORT, NAC/C000355)

Edward Boscawen and Brigadier James Wolfe. With Amherst, Pitt soon realized he had a logistical genius – a methodical general who had proven that he knew how to feed, supply, and move an army. And the British public had a hero. From the Orkney Islands to Land's End, bonfires blazed on hillsides and cannon boomed to celebrate his great victory at Louisbourg. It was the greatest news to come from America since the beginning of the war and the nation spared nothing in its celebration.

Britain would have so many more occasions to celebrate before the year was out that Horace Walpole could facetiously complain that "our bells are worn threadbare with ringing for victories." But that was yet to come as the news from Louisbourg was followed by the news of the disaster at Ticonderoga and the death of Lord Howe. Not until October would Pitt know that Bradstreet had destroyed Fort Frontenac, nor until the New Year that General John Forbes had taken Fort Duquesne.

Pitt's strategic vision still focused on attacking France abroad, rather than her armies in Europe. On December 9, 1758, he wrote to the governors of the northern colonies requesting 20,000 men to be used "for invading Canada by the way of Crown Point, and carrying the War into the Heart of the Enemy's Possessions." To Amherst, he sent a series of more detailed orders directing him to invade Canada by way of lakes George and Champlain; to fortify the Forks of the Ohio; to mount an expedition against Fort Niagara; and to proceed against French posts further west. Pitt also informed Amherst that he had assigned James Wolfe to an independent command that would invade Canada from Louisbourg by way of the lower St. Lawrence "as early in the Year, as on or about, the 7th of May, if the season shall happen to permit."

A legendary figure in Canadian history, General James Wolfe has become known as the man who brought British rule to Canada with his victory at the Plains of Abraham on September 13, 1759. (PAINTING BY JOSEPH HIGHMORE, NAC/C-3916)

Wolfe was an unlikely soldier, a 31-year-old, reed-thin, socially awkward and excitable man who suffered from rheumatism and bladder infections. The son of a lieutenant-general and a controlling, melancholy and self-absorbed mother, he had fought Bonnie Prince Charlie's Highlanders at Culloden in 1746, where he acquired a reputation for recklessness, and served on the Continent with Cumberland. He was ambitious and insecure, but somewhat overwhelmed by the task that Pitt had set him. "I am to act a greater part in this business than I wished or desired," he wrote to an uncle. "I shall do my best and leave the rest to fortune, as perforce we must when there are not the most commanding abilities."

Even Pitt had his doubts, although he was drawn to this strange, young officer whose manic egotism matched his own. At a dinner party at his home before his departure for Canada, Wolfe had left the table and returned with his sword, slashing the air and denouncing his enemies. Pitt, unnerved by this unhinged, impromptu theatre, later commented: "To think that I have committed the fate of my country and my ministry to such hands." Wolfe was not drunk as he had not had much wine that evening and several of Pitt's other guests suggested that he might be mad. However, when King George II heard of the incident, he was elated. "Mad is he?" he said, "then I hope he will bite some of my generals."

Wolfe cleared Spithead on February 14 with a quarter of the British navy, under the command of Admiral Charles Saunders. It was an amazing fleet: 29 ships-of-the-line, 22 frigates, 80 transport ships carrying 20,000 soldiers and sailors, 2000 cannon, 40,000 cannon balls, women, children, prostitutes, and livestock – a floating city with a population larger than

Conducting 49 warships and 119 transports through the treacherous currents and channels of the St. Lawrence, Admiral Sir Charles Saunders led 8,000 troops to Quebec City. (PAINTING BY RICHARD BRAMPTON, PAC/C-121919)

Quebec's. On June 4, a month later than Pitt had wished, after a rendezvous at Louisbourg with additional forces from Halifax, New York, and Boston, the fleet sailed into the St. Lawrence. Instead of the 12,000 troops promised by Pitt, Wolfe would have to make do with fewer than 8000, as many of the American contingents failed to materialize and those did, particularly the Rangers, were men in whom he placed little faith.

As Saunders and his sailing masters and captains plotted their way up the river, the towns and villages along its banks made preparations. "We have settlements on each side of us," wrote John Knox, a captain of the 43rd Regiment aboard HMS *Success.* "The land is uncommonly high above the level of the river, and we see large signal fires everywhere before us... the country-people on the south shore are removing their effects in carts, and conducting them, under escorts of armed men, to a greater distance."

Hoping to discourage the habitants from joining Montcalm at Quebec, Wolfe issued a proclamation: "The formidable sea and land armament which the people of Canada now behold in the heart of your country is intended by the King, my master, to check the insolence of France, to revenge the insults offered to the British colonies, and totally to deprive the French of their most valuable settlement in North America." He had no quarrel with the "industrious peasant," he declared, but if they joined the battle he warned them that they would be mercilessly crushed, their homes and crops destroyed.

On June 27, 1759, the British landed on Île d'Orléans, downriver from Quebec, and Wolfe had his first opportunity to survey the city's defences. It was a discouraging sight. Still, in the presence of his troops he was ener-

Wolfe's attempted landing at Beauport is depicted in this drawing by his aide-de-camp, Captain Harvey Smith. (PAC)

getic, firm, and determined and his headquarters issued reams of orders. But his health began to deteriorate. Almost as soon as he stepped ashore, he "was seized with a fit of the stone and made bloody water." He was melancholy, too, reading constantly from a copy of Thomas Gray's *Elegy Written in a Country Churchyard*, a gift from his fiancée, Katherine Lowther, before he sailed for Canada. "The boasts of heraldry, the pomp of power/ And all that beauty, all that wealth e're gave/Awaits alike the inevitable hour:/The paths of glory lead but to the grave." The passage perfectly suited his presentiment that he would die young.

The defences of Quebec were so seamless that Wolfe could not gain a foothold on the northern shore of the St. Lawrence. So long as provisions held out and Montcalm could shift his forces freely from one part of the line to another, he had little hope of taking the city. He could do little more than shell the city, ravage the countryside, and issue bombastic proclamations calling on the French to surrender. As he wrote to his mother: "My antagonist has wisely shut himself up in inaccessible entrenchments, so that I can't get at him without spilling a torrent of blood, and that perhaps to little purpose. The Marquis de Montcalm is at the head of a great number of bad soldiers and I am at the head of a small number of good ones, that wish for nothing so much as to fight him – but the wary old fellow avoids action doubtful of the behaviour of his army."

The siege of Quebec began on the night of July 12, when a rocket fired from Point Lévis, across the river from the city, briefly lit up the night sky. Batteries of cannon and mortars then kept up a steady barrage until morning. Mother Marie de la Visitation at the General Hospital described the devastation in a letter: "During one night, upwards of fifty of the best houses

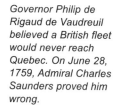

Governor Philip de Rigaud de Vaudreuil believed a British fleet would never reach Quebec. On June 28, 1759, Admiral Charles Saunders proved him wrong.

in the Lower Town were destroyed. The vaults containing merchandise, and many precious articles, did not escape the effects of the artillery. During this dreadful conflagration, we could offer nothing but our tears and prayers at the foot of the altar at such moments as could be snatched from the necessary attention of the wounded."

For the next seven weeks the bombardment continued, slowly reducing the city's fine buildings into charred ruins. "In addition to this misfortune," Marie de la Visitation noted, "we had to contend with more than one enemy; famine, at all times inseparable from war, threatened to reduce us to the last extremity; upwards of six hundred persons in our building and vicinity, partaking of our small means of subsistence, supplied from the government stores, which were likely soon to be short of what was required for the troops… Our enemy, informed of our destitute condition, was satisfied with battering our walls, despairing of vanquishing us, except by starvation."

Throughout July, Wolfe had been unable to dent the city's defences, either by the relentless shelling or the frontal assault on the Beauport lines he had ordered on the last day of the month; an ill-considered attack that cost him 443 casualties, including 210 dead. By the beginning of August, he had run out of ideas and was at odds with his brigadiers James Murray, Robert Monckton, and George Townshend, who had all come to distrust his judgement. He then resorted to terrorism. "I never served so disagreeable a Campaign as this," Townshend wrote to his wife. "Our unequal Force has reduced our Operations to a scene of skirmishing, Cruelty & Desolation. It is War of the Worst Shape. A Scene I ought not to be in… Gen. Wolfe's health is very bad. His generalship, in my poor opinion, is not a bit better, but only between us. He never consulted any of us till the latter end of August, so that we have nothing to answer for…"

By the end of the month, he had reduced the "agreeable prospect of a delightful country" from Kamouraska to Point Lévis to a smoldering waste-land. At Ste-Anne-de-Beaupré, Father Robineau de Portneuf and thirty of his parishioners were taken prisoner, shot, and scalped. At least 23 villages and 1400 farms were destroyed. No one ever tallied the numbers of rapes, scalpings, thefts, and casual murders.

Montcalm had no intention of marching out to defend the villages around Quebec. Indeed, he saw Wolfe's savagery as the work of a desperate com-mander who, having been bloodied at Beauport, shied away "from any sort of landing unless he found absolutely no resistance." Earlier attacks upriver had had a strategic purpose, threatening his supply lines from Montreal and forcing him to assign Bougainville with 3000 troops to patrol the riverbanks. The pillaging downriver served no military purpose whatsoever. As he watched the summer days grow shorter and the nights cooler, he noted in his journal that his enemy's only remaining hope was "a bold stroke, a thunderbolt."

The thunderbolt that Montcalm feared was delivered by Admiral Sir Charles Saunders, when, against all expectations, he sailed ships upriver, beneath the guns of Quebec. Saunders's enterprise became Wolfe's plan. "It will be necessary," he told Saunders, "to run as many small craft as possible by the town… and run us back again in a tide… perhaps we may find an opportunity to strike a blow." Where remained in question.

On September 3, Wolfe, without consulting his brigadiers, abandoned his base on Île d'Orléans and moved his force to the south shore. Surveying the imposing north shore, he decided to land at Anse-au-Foulon, a small cove tucked away under high bluffs about a mile and a half upriver from the city. The cove was one of the few places where the tidal flats were wide enough for troops to land safely. Even better, a path led up from the river's edge to the Plains of Abraham. Wolfe was confident his men could move quickly enough to surprise and overwhelm the French sentries. The Plains were the perfect stage for the set-piece battle he yearned for. If he could marshal his ranks on the Plains, he believed Montcalm would come out and fight.

Montcalm was at Beauport on the morning of September 13, anticipating another British assault, when just after dawn news reached him that Wolfe was on the Plains. Incredulous, he mounted his horse and rode off to see what could be done.

By 8:00 a.m. Wolfe had brought his entire force up the path from Anse-au-Foulon along with two brass fieldpieces. Wheeling his regiments into line as a light rain began to fall, he ordered the men to double shot their muskets for added firepower, then waited calmly for Montcalm to make the next move.

Breasting the slight rise to the west of the city known as the Buttes-à-Neveu, Montcalm was horrified to see a scarlet line of battle running across the whole width of the Plains of Abraham from the St. Charles escarpment down to the cliffs above the St. Lawrence. "I see them where they have no business to be," he told an aide. "This is a serious state of affairs." He immediately decided to bring up his men from the Beauport lines and fight, although they were exhausted from a sleepless night standing watch.

Vaudreuil objected, fearing a second landing at Beauport. He insisted that Montcalm keep his regulars within the walls of the city and wait for Bougainville to close on the British rear. But Montcalm concluded he had no choice but to attack. To his chief of artillery he distractedly said: "We cannot avoid action; the enemy is entrenching, he already has two pieces of cannon. If we give him time to establish himself, we shall never be able to attack him with the sort of troops we have."

Years later, Joseph Trahan, a Canadian militiaman, recalled the scene as Montcalm rode out through the St. Louis Gate. "The marquis was riding a black horse in front of our lines, bearing his sword high in the air. He shouted the question, 'Are you tired?' And we responded with a resounding 'No!' Then, with a 'Vive le Roi!' we advanced."

But the advance was not orderly. Instead of a straight and steady line, some men moved ahead too quickly, while others faltered and fell behind. As Indians and militiamen laid down fire on the flanks, the regulars moved forward in a mix of line and column. When the French artillery opened fire, Wolfe ordered his men to fall to the ground. Shouting and firing on the move, the Canadians, in tried and true frontier fashion, paused to reload, leaving gaps in the line, as the seasoned regulars pressed on.

"The Death of General Wolfe, Quebec." As the British advanced, Wolfe was hit three times, the last shot piercing his chest as his aides and an Indian warrior rushed to his side. Wolfe, who would be immortalized for his victorious campaign, was one of only 58 British fatalities in the final battle at the Plains of Abraham. (PAINTING BY ALONZO CHAPPEL, NAC/ C-042249)

At forty yards, Wolfe ordered his men to their feet. The first rank fired then the second, with devastating effect. "As close and heavy a discharge as I ever saw performed at a private field of exercise," John Knox wrote. Whole regiments went down as the massive volley ripped through them. Then, as a piper struck up "Lovat's March," the Highlanders slung their muskets, unsheathed their claymores, and charged. At the extreme right of the line, Wolfe advanced with the Louisbourg Grenadiers.

After a morning of intermittent rain, the sun broke through as the French fell back helter-skelter for the city and the St. Charles River. Joseph Trahan ran toward the city walls. "I was amongst the fugitives and received in the calf of the leg a spent bullet, which stretched me on the ground," he recalled. "I thought it was all over for me; but presently I rose up and continued to run towards the general hospital, in order to gain the Beauport Camp."

Already wounded in the wrist, an injury he had bound up with a handkerchief, Wolfe suffered a fatal wound, shot through the chest. In shock and hemorrhaging, he clung to consciousness long enough to learn of his victory. Montcalm was wounded moments later, hit by grapeshot, and was carried into the city by two of his officers. When told that he would be dead by morning, Montcalm replied: "Good, I will not see the English in Quebec."

Shortly after 11:00 a.m., Bougainville arrived with his troops, but the battle was over. On the field were 58 British dead and six hundred wounded.

Mortally wounded, French General Louis-Joseph de Montcalm died at daybreak the day after the battle. (ROYAL ONTARIO MUSEUM)

Two hundred and twenty French were dead and hundreds more wounded. Townshend estimated as many as 1500. Equals in death, both the English and French dead were stripped of their uniforms and equipment and buried in common graves on the Plains.

Wolfe, who had achieved the noble death he yearned for, was taken aboard the *Royal William* as the crew stood to attention. His body was preserved in a barrel of rum for the long journey home. Montcalm was buried in a shell hole near the Ursuline convent.

Despite the haze of romance that has come to envelope it, the Plains of Abraham was no more a decisive battle than a brilliant one. Few battles are ever as decisive as generals hope they will be and nowhere was this more true than in Canada. Victories on the battlefield win wars only when the victors retain their conquests. For the British, this was a task which now fell to Murray, Townshend, and Saunders, who immediately set about consolidating control over Quebec and the surrounding countryside, preparing to defend it against the return of the French army.

But mythological heroes were created here. Wolfe, dying at his moment of triumph, immortalized by Benjamin West in the most famous of historical paintings, and the noble Montcalm. And it was here that the epic of French Canada began and ended – in heartbreak and defeat. An unforgotten epic encapsulated in a familiar phrase: "Je me souviens."

⫸ THE DAY AFTER

General James Murray and his troops settle down in a ruined city and brace themselves for winter.

AS WOLFE DAY DYING on the Plains of Abraham, he gave his last order: "Go one of you, my lads, to Colonel Burton. Tell him to march Webb's regiment with all speed down to Charles River to cut off the retreat of the fugitives from the field."

The order was never carried out and his army degenerated into a rabble. Brigadier James Murray took command, fearing Monckton and Townshend were dead. Townshend, very much alive, took over, but instead of pursuing the fleeing French, allowed his men to scavenge the battlefield, robbing the dead, and bayoneting the wounded. Whole battalions moved around without direction, firing at random. French snipers took a toll, and cannons broke up half-hearted attempts to storm the walls. Only the Fraser Highlanders chased the French, howling after them with their claymores until stopped by a murderous fire from the woods at the edge of the plain.

RIGHT: *After Admiral Saunders slipped upstream on the St. Lawrence, Louis-Antoine de Bougainville was forced to patrol 40 miles of shoreline.* (NAC/C-100619)

OPPOSITE PAGE: *Much of Quebec lay in ruins after the heavy bombardment from Saunders' ships. Engraving by Antoine Benoist after a sketch by Richard Short.* (ROYAL ONTARIO MUSEUM)

"I can remember the Scotch Highlanders flying wildly after us with streaming plaids, bonnets and large swords, like so many infuriated demons," Joseph Trahan later wrote. "In their course was a wood, in which we had some Indians and sharpshooters, who bowled them over in fine style. Their partly naked bodies fell on their face, and their kilts in disorder left a large portion of their thighs, at which our fugitives on passing by, would make lunges with their swords, cutting large slices out of the fleshiest portion of their persons."

Other soldiers dug trenches and fortified houses on the Sillery and Ste. Foy roads while sailors hauled big naval guns up the Anse-au-Foulon. Burial parties set to work. "All along the battlefield on the Plains," a nun wrote, "still reeking of blood and covered with the slain, the victors were opening the turf to hide from view the hideous effects of war." Over the next three days, Townshend lost 36 men to cannon fire from the city walls – a considerable number as only 58 had been killed in the actual battle.

In the city, confusion reigned supreme. Montcalm was sinking slowly from a wound to the groin, his surgeons telling him he had less than twelve hours to live. Painfully, he dictated three courses of action to an aide. The governor, he said, could reform the army and counterattack; he could retreat by an inland route to Jacques-Cartier; or, he could surrender the colony. He, Montcalm, would not suggest which course to take. "I will neither give orders nor interfere any further," he told Jean-Baptiste-Nicolas-Roch de Ramezay, the garrison commander. "I have much business that must be attended to, of greater moment than your ruined garrison and this wretched country. My time is short, therefore pray leave me." He died at daybreak, just 24 hours after Wolfe appeared on the Plains of Abraham.

Governor Pierre de Rigaud de Vaudreuil noted that French officers were "indisposed to battle." A council of war decided to abandon Quebec without informing the civilian population. The army marched out at nine o'clock on the night of September 13, leaving guns, ammunition, and food supplies behind. "It was not a retreat," a witness recalled, "but a horrid, abominable flight, 1000 times worse than that in the morning upon the Heights of Abraham. By six the next morning, they were safely at Lorette, their flanks protected by Bougainville's troops. Lévis, the tough Gascon brigadier who had assumed command following Montcalm's death, stiffened their spines, showing nothing but scorn for their hasty retreat. With reinforcements and supplies from France, this very capable soldier was confident he could re-take the city.

Meanwhile, at the hospital, nuns were trying to care for the sick and wounded. "We were surrounded by the dead and dying who were brought in by the hundreds," Mother St. Ignace remembered. "Many of them were closely connected with us, but we had to lay aside our grief and seek for space in which to put them." A British guard was later placed around the hospital and Townshend came to reassure the nuns that the wounded would not be harmed.

Ramezay was given draft articles of surrender to use when his food ran out or when the British stormed the walls. Stores left behind in the Beauport Lines could have fed the 6000 civilians left behind in Quebec for weeks, but they were looted by Indians during the night. "Despondency was complete," Ramezay wrote, "discouragement extreme and universal. Murmurs and complaints against the army that abandoned them rose to a general outcry." The mayor and prominent citizens signed a petition demanding surrender and a reluctant Ramezay ran up a white flag.

On the morning of September 18, 1759, Townshend and Saunders formally signed the surrender. The terms were generous, for the British were far too weak to impose order on the city and its people. For the only time after the massacre at Fort William Henry, a defeated French garrison was permitted to surrender with the honours of war. The regulars were not to be made prisoners of war, but rather transported under a flag of truce to

France, where they would be free to rejoin the French army. Militiamen could remain with their families, provided they surrender their weapons and swear an oath of fidelity to the British Crown. Anyone willing to take the oath would enjoy all the protection normally afforded to British subjects. Property rights would be respected, "the free exercise of Roman religion" guaranteed, the bishop of Quebec and the clergy protected, and soldiers would be sent to guard churches and convents.

That evening, 50 artillerymen entered the St. Louis Gate pulling a gun carriage bearing the British colours. The Louisbourg Grenadiers took post while naval parties landed in Lower Town and Townshend and his staff marched to the Chateau St. Louis, Champlain's fortress on the rock. A line of French troops was drawn up before the ruined walls as Ramezay stepped forward to hand Townshend the ceremonial keys to the city. And from the river below came the crash of a victory salvo by the guns of the fleet.

If England had blazed with a thousand bonfires with the fall of Louisbourg, ten thousand lit the night skies when word spread that Quebec, too, had fallen. The news arrived in London almost at the same time it reached Amherst on Lake Champlain, and by then Pitt had almost given up hope. In his last gloomy dispatches, Wolfe had brooded on his failures and confessed that he was "at a loss how to determine" his next move. "I am so far recovered in health as to do business," his final letter read, "but my constitution is entirely ruined, without the consolation of having done any considerable service to the State, or without any prospect of it." Now, as he read the letter in which Townshend described the battle on the Plains of Abraham and the surrender of the city, his mood swung to exaltation. So, too, did the country's.

That Wolfe had died in battle only made his victory richer for the more sentimentally inclined. "The incidents of dramatic fiction could not be conducted with more address to lead an audience from despondency to sudden exultation," Horace Walpole wrote. "The whole people of Britain despaired – they triumphed – and they wept – for Wolfe had fallen in the hour of victory! Joy, grief, curiosity, astonishment were painted in every countenance: the more they inquired, the higher their admiration rose. Not an incident but was heroic and effecting! ...Ancient history may be ransacked, and ostentatious philosophy thrown into account, before an episode can be

The French army retreated up the St. Lawrence to the fortified town of Montreal after their defeat at the Plains of Abraham until the next year when Governor Vaudreuil signed the capitulation of New France.

found to rank with Wolfe's."

In New England there were so many bonfires that they were said to dim the moon and an "Abundance of extraordinary Fire-Works that play'd off in almost every Street; more especially the greatest Quantity of Sky-Rockets ever seen on any Occasion." There were sermons aplenty, attributing Wolfe's victory to divine providence. "We have received a Salvation from Heaven, greater perhaps than any since the Foundations of the Country," said the Reverend Samuel Cooper of Boston. A sentiment shared in New York and Philadelphia.

But there was little to celebrate in Quebec in this year of victories, Walpole's Annus Mirabilis. Quebec was a shambles. More than 500 houses had been destroyed with Lower Town a maze of roofless walls. In Upper Town, the cathedral was a blackened shell and Mountain Street a rubble-strewn path with the gaunt remains of the bishop's palace, and Jesuit and Récollet churches clinging to its slope. When Monckton and Townshend sailed for home, Brigadier James Murray, the military governor was left with 7000 men, only 5000 of whom were fit. Every available man was put to work clearing the streets and strengthening the fortifications, for Murray knew that an attack must come.

Murray, a 40-year-old Scot and the most junior of Wolfe's brigadiers, was popular with the Canadians. By mid-winter, nearly 8000 had come into the city, surrendering their arms and swearing allegiance to the King of England. They seemed more bitter towards Montcalm, Vaudreuil, and Bigot than the English. The ladies of Quebec took pains to teach the officers French, prompting a cynical lieutenant to suspect that they wanted to hear

Notre-Dame-de-la-Victoire, the church built to celebrate Frontenac's 1690 defence of the city, lay in ruins in 1760. (NAC/C-025662)

themselves praised in their own language.

While the officers flirted in the few remaining drawing rooms, the men froze to death in the streets and in the ruins that served as barracks. Daily work parties dressed in any clothing they could find – habitant shirts, discarded French uniforms, or scraps of fur – cut logs for firewood, carrying them back on sleighs. After an ice storm in January, the kilted Frasers reached their guard posts in Lower Town by sliding down Mountain Street on bare behinds. The city's nuns immediately set to work knitting long woolen underwear for the frostbitten Highlanders.

"Our guards, on the grande parade, make a most grotesque appearance in their different dresses," John Knox wrote, "and our inventions to guard us against the extreme vigour of this climate are various beyond imagination: the uniformity, as well as the nicety, of the clean, methodical soldier, is buried in the rough fur-wrought garb of the frozen Laplander."

Sentries died at their posts as the fierce Canadian winter set in. Thanks to Wolfe laying waste the countryside the previous summer, there was no fresh food, only salt pork, and scurvy swept through the garrison. One hundred and fifty men were dead by Christmas and the toll would reach 1000 by the end of April. Hundreds of bodies lay unburied. Rum, which was readily available, helped many to survive, but it also brought drunken rampages through the streets, looting, robbery, and rape. Women who sold rum without permission were stripped to the waist and whipped. Several men were shot or hanged. In one case two were condemned, but Murray decided that only one need die. They threw dice to decide and the loser was executed. Men caught trying to desert were given 1000 lashes. Successful deserters were more often than not captured by the French. "The English were not safe beyond the gates of Quebec," Marie de la Visitation wrote. "General Murray, the commander of the place, on several occasions was near being made a prisoner; and would not have escaped if our people had not been faithful … we heard of nothing but combats throughout the winter; the severity of the season had not the effect of making them lay down their arms."

While Murray's men froze to death at their posts or were lost to "fevers, dysenteries, and most obstinate scorbutic disorders," Lévis and Vaudreuil, in their comfortable quarters in Montreal, were laying plans for a spring offensive to retake Quebec. The odds were heavily against them and neither the governor nor the general had any illusions about their chances of success. Their only hope was to strike quickly in the spring before the British could bring reinforcements up the river. Once Murray was defeated, they reasoned, they could turn against Amherst's army coming up Lake Champlain and the Richelieu River. They could expect little help from France, which was teetering towards bankruptcy.

Murray watched their movements carefully. Faced with imminent attack, he called in his outposts and consolidated his forces in Quebec. At the same time, fearing that civilians within the city might act as a fifth column, he ordered them expelled. Having done nothing to warrant this treatment, they marched bitterly through the St. Louis Gate into the ravaged countryside, cursing the lying and faithless English.

Spring arrived late in 1760, and Lévis did not leave Montreal with his army until April 20. As the expedition made its way down the St. Lawrence, the villagers along the river offered cheers and prayers, but were reluctant to surrender their young men, most of whom had deserted from the militia the previous fall and sworn allegiance to the Crown. By this time, the French soldier cared nothing for Canada, and the Canadian soldier cared little for France. "What a country," Bougainville wrote, "and what patience is needed to bear slights that people go out of their way to lay on us here. It seems as though we belonged to a different nation, even a hostile one."

Five days later, Lévis and his army landed at St. Augustin and by the following day were at Cap Rouge River, a few miles upstream from Quebec. That night, according to John Knox, there was "violent thunder and lightning surpassing any thing of the kind that has been known in this country for many years; and was succeeded by a most tremendous storm of wind and rain… the river was so agitated by this uncommon storm as effectually to tear up and disperse all the remaining ice." Soon afterwards, the crew of the *Racehorse* pulled a half-starved man from an ice flow. He turned out to be a sergeant of the French artillery, the sole survivor of a bateau that had overturned in the storm. Fortified with rum, he told his captors that Lévis was on his way to Sillery with 7000 men.

Although Murray could muster fewer than 3800 troops, he decided that he would march out to meet him. He explained to Pitt: "The enemy was greatly superior in numbers, it is true; but when I considered that our little army was in the habit of beating that enemy, and had a very fine train of field artillery; that shutting ourselves at once within the walls was putting all upon the single chance of holding out for a considerable time a wretched fortification, I resolved to give them battle."

Early on the morning of April 28, Murray's infantry – every man healthy enough to shoulder a musket – marched through the St. Louis Gate. Some carried entrenching tools; others were harnessed to pull artillery as all the horses had starved or been eaten during the winter. Like Montcalm seven months before, he formed ranks on the Plains of Abraham – on the commanding ridge along the Buttes-à-Neveu. Murray intended to dig in, an unlikely proposition as much of the ground was still frozen.

Looking south, Murray could see skirmishers approaching through the woods at Sillery, while Lévis's main force advanced close to the Ste. Foy road. Impulsively deciding to attack, he ordered his men to stop digging, fix bayonets, and advance on the French before they had time to deploy. By doing so, he gave up his chief advantage – position – and by moving down from the high ground, he lost the advantage of his artillery. John Knox recalled that "we were insensibly drawn from our advantageous situation into low swampy ground, where our troops fought almost knee-deep in dissolving wreaths of snow and water!"

Lévis saw that Murray meant to give battle and ordered his vanguard back. "A movement," he wrote, "which was carried out with the greatest bravery and activity under a heavy artillery and musket fire!" Interpreting the movement as a retreat, Murray ordered a charge to seize Dumont's

François-Gaston de Lévis was considered by many as the outstanding European general to serve on either side during the Seven Years War. On Montcalm's death, he took over command. Although he experienced some initial success in his attempt to retake Quebec, he was ultimately defeated in 1760 after he received no support from France. (NAC/C-009141)

Mill and its outbuildings, which commanded the Ste. Foy road. Lévis calmly ordered his centre to hold firm, then counterattacked on the British flanks. In fierce hand-to-hand combat, Murray's men fought desperately to prevent their flanks from being enveloped. Dumont's Mill changed hands several times until French Grenadiers prevailed. The Highlanders and Rangers companies were almost completed destroyed after three hours of fighting, allowing the Royal Roussillon Regiment to march forward and lay down a deadly enfilading fire on the British left. It crumbled. Murray later wrote: "Disorder spread from left to right and the whole retired… abandoning their cannon to the enemy."

Murray ordered a withdrawal, which turned into disorderly retreat. Without horses the artillery could not be moved out of harm's way and more than twenty guns were left to the French. In the meantime, Lévis ordered one of his regiments to sweep around the British. In the fog of battle, however, the order went awry and the British were able to reach the safety of the city's walls. Murray later claimed that he was the last British soldier to leave the field. Even his loyal quartermaster complained of his "mad, enthusiastic zeal," noting that "we were too few and weak to launch an assault and we were in almost as deep distress as we could be … half starved, scorbutic skeletons."

Murray's ill-considered attack had cost him 1104 officers and men, including 259 dead – five times the number in the September battle. Lévis recorded his losses at 833 with 93 killed.

"The jubilation here is unparalleled," Bougainville reported from the Île-aux-Noix, as Lévis landed cannon at Anse-au-Foulon and dragged them

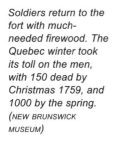

Soldiers return to the fort with much-needed firewood. The Quebec winter took its toll on the men, with 150 dead by Christmas 1759, and 1000 by the spring.
(*NEW BRUNSWICK MUSEUM*)

up the path that Wolfe had climbed to besiege the city. Both sides knew the outcome depended on support from Britain or France and that the flag of the first ship up the river would determine the outcome.

There was outrage in London. Walpole wrote caustically: "Who the deuce was thinking of Quebec! Canada was like a book one has read and done with, and here we were suddenly reading our book backwards!"

In Quebec, Murray's men were bitter. Captain Charles Stewart of the Fraser Highlanders, lying wounded in his quarters remarked to fellow officers: "From April battles and Murray's generals, good Lord deliver me!" Lieutenant Malcolm Fraser of the same regiment wrote: "The General has every military virtue except prudence!"

By May 11, with his lines complete and his guns in place, Lévis was ready to begin the bombardment of Quebec. Although the British could respond with twenty rounds to every one Lévis could afford to fire from his meager stock of ammunition, Murray had only enough provisions to hold on for about two weeks. If relief did not reach him before then he would be forced to capitulate.

Lévis's situation was a little better. In November, he had sent his chief of artillery Le Mercier off to Paris to plead for help at court. Had he known the miserable results of Mercier's mission, he would have despaired. Not only was his plea ignored, he was arrested and charged with fraud and embezzlement. Then, in a gesture that came too late, Paris sent a pitiful convoy of five merchantmen accompanied by a single warship to Quebec. They made it as far as the mouth of the St. Lawrence before a British patrol out of Halifax took them as prizes.

At 11 o'clock on the morning of May 9, French pickets above Anse-au-Foulon and the English defenders on Cape Diamond saw a vessel round the point of Île d'Orléans. For a few moments, she was thought to be French and there was a shout of "Vive le Roi!" then the Union Jack broke from her maintop and she fired a salute as the troops on the walls, Murray among them, went wild. She was the frigate *Lowestoft*, veteran of many wars. A week later, the *Vanguard* and *Diana* arrived and Lévis gave up the siege, complaining in a letter to Paris that "one single frigate" would have given him Quebec and saved Canada for another year.

Carrying what they could on their backs, Lévis's men scrambled on board their boats and rowed for their lives as *Vanguard* and *Diana* opened fire on the French lines. The French frigate *Pomone* ran aground while trying to cover the retreat, leaving the *Atalante* to stand off the British warships. Captain Jean Vauquelin, the master of the only ship to escape Louisbourg in 1758, nailed his colours to the mast and shot it out with his pursuers until his gunners ran out of ammunition. Wounded but still defiant, he ordered his crew to abandon ship, and waited on his quarterdeck for the British to take him prisoner.

Vauquelin's fate and that of his ship foretold what lay in store for Lévis and French Canada. From now on, Lévis would be on the defensive and his hopes limited to finding some last gesture by which he could temper defeat with honour. Like Vauquelin and the crew of the *Atalante*, neither Lévis's audacity nor his soldiers' courage, could stop the approaching juggernaut.

LEFT: *On April 28, 1760, Murray left the safety of Quebec City's fortifications to meet Lévis's forces. Outnumbered, the British were forced back into the fort, abandoning 20 field pieces in the process.* (NAC)

OPPOSITE PAGE: *An illustration of Ottawa chief Pontiac taking up the war hatchet in 1763.* (GRANGER COLLECTION, 4E233.12)

❧ PONTIAC'S REBELLION

Abandoned by their French allies, defeated and despised, the Native tribes of the northwest rally around an obscure Ottawa war chief.

IT WOULD BE DIFFICULT to overstate General Jeffrey Amherst's visceral dislike for Indians or his ignorance of their culture. The Indians, he told an aide, must be treated "as the vilest Race of Beings that ever Infested the Earth and whose Riddance from it must be esteemed a Meritorious Act, for the good of mankind." In the spring of 1763, when news reached his headquarters in New York that the western tribes had besieged Detroit, he suggested they should be infected with smallpox and hunted down with dogs. "It is a pity to oppose Good men against them," he wrote. "I wish we could make use of the Spaniard's method and hunt them with English Dogs." Spreading smallpox, shooting women and children, and murdering prisoners – all became part of Amherst's plan to pacify the frontier.

Native allies of the French gather for some friendly bow and arrow competition in preparation for battle against the British. By the mid-18th century, many Natives in that area had obtained rifles from Pennsylvania Dutch craftsmen. These muskets outclassed the Brown Bess used by the British in both range and accuracy. (LIBRARY OF CONGRESS)

At Fort Pitt, Captain Simeon Ecuyer, a Swiss mercenary, had anticipated Amherst. When a group of Ottawa and Delaware chiefs arrived at the fort to parley, Ecuyer heard them out, then presented them with a parting "gift" – two blankets and a handkerchief taken from the smallpox hospital which had been cut into pieces and placed in small tin boxes. The chiefs were told the boxes contained medicine and they should not open them until they were home.

Andrew Blackbird, the adopted son of an Ottawa chief, left this account of what happened when they were opened:

"Accordingly, after they reached home they opened the box; but behold there was another tin box inside, smaller. They took it out and opened the second box, and behold, still there was another box inside the second box, smaller yet. So they kept on this way till they came to a very small box, which was not more than an inch long; and when they opened the last one they found nothing but mouldy particles in this last box... Pretty soon burst out a terrible sickness among them. The great Indian doctors themselves were taken sick and died. The tradition says that it was indeed awful and terrible. Everyone taken with it was sure to die. Lodge after lodge was totally vacated—nothing but dead bodies lying here and there in their lodges. The whole coast of Arbor Croche ... which is said to have been a continuous village some fifteen or sixteen miles long ... was entirely depopulated and laid waste."

All this had been sadly prophetic to Pontiac, an obscure Ottawa war chief who the summer before had seized on a divine message delivered to the Abenaki: "I warn you that if you allow the English among you, you are

Even as he was gathering his forces for the attacks on Fort Detroit, Pontiac sought to allay Major Henry Gladwin's suspicions as depicted in this painting, where Pontiac and three other Ottawa chiefs meet with the fort's commander. The attack was launched the following day. (BURTON HISTORICAL COLLECTION)

dead; maladies, smallpox and their poison will destroy you totally..."

In the spring of 1763, after the French had officially withdrawn from the western territories—the fabled *pays d'en haut*—English fur traders, hunters, and backwoods settlers moved in, in ever increasing numbers, to occupy the French forts and trading posts. So many in the valleys of the Monongahela, Loyalhanna, and Allegheny rivers that the commandant of Fort Pitt found it necessary to issue a proclamation forbidding settlement except where specifically authorized. Eventually, he ordered the houses of squatters burned. But nothing could stem the tide.

Fort Pitt and even the smaller settlements that grew up at Niagara, Fort Stanwix, Detroit, and other frontier forts were larger and more intrusive than any French trading post had ever been. The French were traders and soldiers; they inhabited the land the way the Indians did, lightly and seasonally. The English, on the other hand, were settlers who marked the land into grids, cultivated and settled it, felled tracts of forest for fuel and building materials, planted fields of corn and beans, built houses, barns, stores, warehouses, and schools for their children. Indian leaders understood only too well that the settlers had not come to trade and live peacefully among them.

To make matters worse, Amherst discontinued the French practice of bestowing gifts to the Indians and would not sell them rum. "I do not see why the Crown should be put to the expense of supporting the Indians," he told an aide. "As to the purchasing of good behaviour either of Indians, or any Others, is what I do not understand; when men of what race soever behave ill, they must be punished but not bribed."

Defeated and despised, many Indians turned to spiritual leaders for solace. Prophets arose. Among the most influential was Neolin "the Enlightened," a Delaware who rejected servile acceptance of English rule and preached resistance to the "dogs clothed in red."

At Fort Michilimakinac, Ojibwa Chief Minweweh spoke of a war that never ended. "Englishman, although you have conquered the French you have not yet conquered us!" he defiantly told English traders. "We are not your slaves. These lakes, these woods and mountains were left us by our ancestors. They are our inheritance; and we will part with them to none..."

Pontiac was familiar with the teachings of Neolin and Minweweh. Major Robert Rogers, the vainglorious and self-publicizing leader of Ranger units that were supposed to replace the Indian allies the British lacked, had met Pontiac two years before, when Amherst sent him to accept the surrender of the French posts in the west. Rogers was impressed with the chief and described him as a man "greatly honoured and revered by his subjects." He also noted that he was "proud, vindictive, warlike, and easily offended."

Making no secret of his discontentment with Amherst's trade and settlement policies, Pontiac spent the winter of 1762-63 rallying the tribes from the Great Lakes to the Gulf of Mexico. On May 5, 1763, he addressed hundreds of Ottawa, Huron, and Potawatomi in a grand council.

"It is important for us, my brothers, that we exterminate from our lands this nation which seeks only to destroy us," he told them. "...All the nations who are our brothers attack them—why should we not attack? Are we not men like them?"

Pontiac's rebellion began at Detroit when the Ottawa, Potawatomi, Huron and a band of Chippewa attacked soldiers and settlers outside its walls. Robert Navarre, a French notary, observed the gruesome scene:

"The savages disembarked their prisoners, one company after another, upon the stand and made them strip naked, and other Indians then discharged their arrows into all parts of their bodies... The poor victims had to keep standing till they fell dead in their tracks and those who had not engaged in the killing fell upon them. Some they treated with different cruelty, slashing them alive with gun-flints, stabbing them with spears, cutting off their hands and feet and letting them bathe in their own blood and die in agony; others were bound to stakes and burned by children in a slow fire."

Messengers raced from village to village across the *pays d'en haut* carrying news of the attack on Detroit. As if by pre-arrangement, other tribes took up the hatchet against remote thinly manned outposts. On May 16, Wyandot warriors surprised and seized Fort Sandusky. Nine days later, the Potawatomi captured Fort St. Joseph. Fort Miami (now Fort Wayne, Indiana) fell to the local Miami on the 27th. Flushed with victory, the Miami persuaded the Kickapoo, Macouten, and Wea to join them and seized Fort Ouiaternon. At Michilimakinac, on the strait between lakes Huron and Michigan, Chippewa that were pretending to play a game of lacrosse gained entry to the fort by a classic ruse. Throwing the ball inside the stockade, a player ran through the gate to retrieve it, followed by a group of spectators, mostly women. Once inside, the women drew concealed weapons from their clothes and passed them to the men. In a matter of minutes they nearly annihilated the garrison. Every post in the west was overrun, with the exception of Niagara, Fort Pitt, and Detroit.

Amherst's reaction to the news from the west bordered on fury. He told Colonel Henry Bouquet, commanding a relief force marching to Fort Pitt, to "put every Indian in your Power to Death." Fortunately, he was about to be replaced as commander-in -chief by General Thomas Gage, a more humane man, who had first come to America with MGen. Edward Braddock in 1755.

Marching via forts Loudoun, Bedford, and Ligonier, Bouquet and his force, loaded down with provisions for the besieged garrison, fought their way through to Fort Pitt on August 10. To the north, Pontiac continued to press on Detroit, but his coalition of tribes was fragile. As it became increasingly apparent that the fort would not fall, individual chiefs struck deals with the British and headed home.

With his power waning and abandoned by the French who advised him to make peace, Pontiac dictated a note to Major Gladwin, the commanding officer of Fort Detroit. "My Brother," he wrote, "The word which my father has sent me to make peace I have accepted; all my young men have buried their hatchets. I think you will forget the bad things which have taken place for some time past. Likewise I forget what you may have done to me, in order to think of nothing but good. I, the Chippewa, the Huron, we are ready to speak with you when you ask us."

But Gladwin refused to speak to him and Gage, determined to crush the uprising once and for all, dispatched a large force under the command of Colonel John Bradstreet, another veteran of Braddock's ill-fated march to the Monongahela, "to give peace to all such nations of Indians as would sue for it, and chastise those that continued in arms." Pontiac broke camp and headed south while the Shawnee, Delaware, Wyandot and Mingo chiefs met Bradstreet and assured him of their sincere desire for peace. Bradstreet granted them amnesty, a policy which ran counter to Amherst's desire for revenge and won him few friends among his superiors.

The following spring, Pontiac travelled to Oswego with chiefs of the Ottawa, Potawatomi, Huron, and Chippewa for a grand peace council with William Johnson, the Superintendent for Indian Affairs in the Northern Department, and the chiefs of the Six Nations. The council lasted for nine days, and the "Western Nations" embraced the "Chain of Friendship" after an exchange of belts and gifts. Pontiac returned to his home a marked man, the western chiefs angry that he had led them into a war they could not win. According to Johnson, a French trader from Detroit "offered to lay me a bet that Pontiac would be killed in less than a year."

On April 20, 1769, Pontiac walked into Baynton, Wharton and Morgan's general store in Cahokia, not far from his home on the banks of the Mississippi, opposite present-day St. Louis, Missouri. He engaged in friendly conversation with neighbours, made a few purchases, then left. A Peoria Indian who had been standing by the counter followed him into the street and without warning clubbed him from behind with an axe handle, then stabbed him to death.

News of Pontiac's assassination spread quickly. So, too, did conspiracy theories—most of them alleging some sort of British involvement. Nothing was ever proved, and to the surprise of nearly everyone, none of the western tribes took revenge. For the first time in decades, the frontier was relatively quiet as the British consolidated their power and the Indians watched and waited—and died of smallpox.

OPPOSITE PAGE: *Sir Jeffrey Amherst took Louisbourg in 1758 and then captured Montreal in 1760, effectively ending French rule in Canada.*

SIC GLORIA TRANSIT

Although celebrated in his lifetime as the conqueror of Canada, Jeffrey Amherst was soon forgotten.

CHEVALIER AUGUSTIN DE BOSCHENRY de Drucour, governor of Louisbourg from 1754 until its surrender in 1758, thought he could conduct a campaign according to a medieval code of knightly virtues. So too did his wife, who walked the ramparts daily to fire a cannon to encourage the besieged troops. Amherst, duly impressed, sent her two pineapples fresh from the Azores accompanied by an appropriately gallant note. Madame replied with a crate of champagne which prompted more pineapples and a firkin of butter while her husband offered the services of a noted physician on his staff to wounded British officers. But such Old World gallantries could not save the fortress, and Louisbourg duly surrendered. On Pitt's orders, Louisbourg was to be "totally demolished, and razed, and all the materials so thoroughly destroyed, as that no use may, hereafter, be ever made of the same."

The garrison and the citizens of Louisbourg were deported to France. Drucour was disgraced for surrendering the fortress. He died four years later in poverty. His wife, Marie-Anne, "La Bombardière," died two months later.

In London, the French colours captured at Louisbourg were paraded through the streets and deposited in St. Paul's Cathedral as church bells rang to celebrate the first British victory in three years of hostilities. Parliament expressed its thanks and Amherst's troops were granted an advance of pay of one shilling to drink his Majesty's health. Amherst was rewarded with an appointment as commander-in-chief of all British forces in North America.

Jeffrey Baron Amherst, a Guards officer with a 23-year record of distinguished service, had as a boy served as a page to the Duke of Dorset. Instead of following the family tradition of the Law and the Church, he decided on an army career and, thanks to the Duke's patronage, obtained an ensign's commission in the 1st Regiment of Foot Guards. Serving on the Continent with the Duke of Cumberland, he was rapidly promoted. He fought at Dettingen and Fontenoy as a regimental commander, then took command of a brigade. On March 3, 1758, Pitt presented "his compliments to Major General Amherst and sends him here with His Majesty's commission to command at the Siege of Louisbourg." Celebrated in his lifetime, he is largely forgotten now, his accomplishments overshadowed by those of his subordinate – James Wolfe.

Drucour's valiant defence of Louisbourg had saved Canada for another year. It was now too late in the season for Amherst to move up the St. Lawrence to coordinate an attack with Abercrombie's push up Lake Champlain and the Richelieu. It was also too late for Abercrombie. Decisively defeated by Montcalm at Ticonderoga, he fell back on Albany where he was relieved of his command. Wolfe, in the meantime, lay waste to the Gaspé, reporting to Amherst that "we have done a great deal of mischief and spread the terror of His Majesty's arms but have added nothing to the reputation of them."

Amherst, his reputation in the ascendant, moved on to Boston after entertaining the Drucours aboard HMS *Terrible*. "I had decided to have no ceremony," he wrote on September 15, 1758, "but the whole Town turned out and I was received by the principal people." His troops disembarked the following day, which was declared a day of thanksgiving. "Rum was much too plenty," he complained. "When we marched out I had to leave the Quarter-Guards of every regiment to take care of the drunks and bring them up when sober." Supply wagons and baggage trundling along behind them, they continued on to Albany.

Like Braddock, Loudoun, and Abercrombie before him, Amherst had little use for the colonial troops under his command. "The provincials," he wrote, "have got home in their heads & will no do very little good. I hear they are deserting from every Post where I have been obliged to leave some & several ran away who had a good deal of money due to them. Twill be so much saved to the Publick." He had already formed an unshakable opinion: "The Disregard of Orders, and Studying of their own Ease, rather than the good of the Service, has been too often Just Grounds for Complaint Against Some of the Provincial Officers, and all their Men." They no more than a necessary evil, he thought, settled on him by the need for labourers and garrison troops. Holding them in as much contempt as he did the Indians, he would never think of them as soldiers, and could hardly wait to put them and "their wretched country," behind him. His inability to understand the Indians as anything but barbaric, would have serious consequences for his later career in North America.

Amherst has been criticized for being overcautious, which no doubt he was. Formal and aloof, he inspired respect, but not affection, in his subordinates. His most important brigadier, James Wolfe, found him maddeningly uncommunicative and "slow." His plodding advance and failure to create a diversion for Wolfe at Quebec have come under attack, as have his laborious fort and road building along Lake Champlain. However, he did much useful work improving communications, and his decision to build a fort at Crown Point was not only of military importance, it also allowed displaced settlers to return to their homes and colonize the country between Fort Edward and Lake George. Moreover, his command was marked by success. He contributed to that success by occupying Ticonderoga and Crown Point; by sending expeditions under brigadiers John Forbes, John Prideaux, and William Johnson to capture Fort Duquesne and Niagara; and by carrying out a converging movement of forces on Montreal which resulted in the capture of the city in 1760.

"I have come to take Canada and I do not intend to take anything else," he informed the governor, the Marquis de Vaudreuil, and so he did. With some justification he later wrote: "I believe never three Army's setting out from different and distant parts from each other, joined in the Centre, as was intended, better than we did, and it could not fail of having the effect of which I have just now seen the consequences."

Amherst, Murray, and Colonel William de Haviland joined forces on September 6, 1760, a few miles outside the city. Their progress had almost been a triumphant excursion, although Amherst lost 84 men in the Lachine Rapids, more than he had lost to enemy action in the entire campaign.

Neither the walls of Montreal nor the garrison within were sufficient to offer more than token resistance to the British. Most of the militia and the Indians had already left, and even some of the regulars had deserted. As Amherst's engineers planned the siege, Vaudreuil, Lévis and Bigot discussed surrender. They had barely 3,000 men. Although the situation was hopeless, Vaudreuil opted to play for time, sending Bougainville to offer Amherst conditions: a one-month ceasefire until it could be ascertained whether peace had already been concluded in Europe. Amherst replied that the French had until noon the following day to surrender. Vaudreuil finally agreed to a full and complete surrender. The terms were generous and allowed French troops, both the Troupes de la Marine et la Terre, the right to parole to France, where they could continue to serve their King. Amherst agreed to a surprising number of the conditions that Vaudreuil had proposed. In one particular, however, Amherst was firm. He refused to offer his foe the "honours of war," accusing the French of exciting "the savages to perpetrate the most horrid and unheard of barbarities." Lévis and his fellow officers were stung. In a final act of defiance, he broke the blade of his sword rather than surrender it and ordered the regimental colours burned.

On September 9, Amherst, with Vaudreuil in attendance, marched his victorious troops through the streets of Montreal to the Place d'Armes for the formal surrender, which included all the troops in Canada. Returning in triumph to New York, he was immediately appointed governor general of British North America.

In Britain, news of Amherst's victory was greeted with fireworks, bonfires, artillery salutes, the ringing of church bells and thanksgiving services. The French were defeated, but victory had come at a great cost. In this the first world war, the forces of England, France, and their allies fought on virtually every continent. Thousands of soldiers and sailors had died in Europe and on the high seas, with many thousands more in North America, the Caribbean, Africa, and India. Never before had nations warred on such a scale. England had triumphed and its war leaders had acquired vast new territories, including Canada with its 65,000 French-speaking inhabitants.

Knighted, Amherst returned home to tend to a mad wife, his languishing estate, and fleeting fame as the greatest military administrator since the death of the Duke of Marlborough and the rise of Wellington.

It was only after his return, however, that he realized that he been summoned – not to be celebrated as the conqueror of Canada, but to be blamed for a rebellion that, in his own mind at least, had come out of thin air.

RIGHT: *A panoramic view of Louisbourg in August 1744. A cloud of smoke rises from a careened shipt.* (RECONSTITUTION BY LEWIS PARKER, FORTRESS LOUISBOURG, CANADIAN PARKS SERVICE)

BELOW: *Thanks to Sir Jeffrey Amherst's successful siege, the capture of Louisbourg, the French fortress on Cape Breton Island, on July 28, 1758, opened the St. Lawrence for Admiral Charles Saunders and his fleet. Under the overall command of General James Wolfe, the British ships would make Quebec City their next objective.* (MARY EVANS PICTURE LIBRARY)

TIMELINE OF KEY EVENTS

1000 Vikings land on shores of New-foundland

1006 First skirmishes between Norsemen and the 'skrellings.'

1492 Columbus "discovers" North America.

1497 Giovanni Caboto (John Cabot) lands on North American coast.

1534 Cartier claims Canada as "New France."

1604 Pierre de Monts founds Canada's first colony at Port Royal, NS.

1608 Champlain founds Quebec City.

1613 Champlain drives Iroquois from St. Lawrence Valley. English raids on French on Bay of Fundy.

1618 – 1648 Thirty Years War. Continent of Europe devastated by shifting alliances and religious strife.

1626 – 1630 Anglo-French War spreads to colonies.

1629 Settlement of Quebec captured by British privateers, the Kirke brothers.

1635 Aged 65, Champlain dies in Quebec.

1632 Treaty of Saint-Germaine-en-Laye returns New France to French.

1642 De Maisonneuve founds Ville-Marie (Montreal).

1649 Jesuits burn and abandon Sainte-Marie among the Hurons following Iroquois attacks.

1652 – 1654 Anglo-Dutch War. Firearms introduced to Indians by European powers. British seize Long Island.

1660 Iroquois besiege Dollard des Ormeaux near Carillon, Quebec.

1654 New Englanders seize Acadia (restored to France in 1670).

1664 – 1667 Second Anglo-Dutch War. Britain takes New Amsterdam (New York).

1670 Hudson Bay Company receives Royal Charter in London.

1675 King Philip's War ravages New England.

1686 – 1697 D'Iberville rules over Hudson Bay

1689 Lachine Massacre starts new series of Iroquois raids.

1689 – 1697 King William's War (War of the League of Augsburg)

1690 Capture of Port Royal by New Englanders

1692 Madeleine de Verchères defends

family fort against Iroquois.

1696 Frontenac subdues Iroquois.

1697 Treaty of Ryswick ends King William's War; Newfoundland and Hudson Bay ceded to Britain, Acadia to France

1701 French occupy Spanish Netherlands; Grand Alliance (Britain, Netherlands, Austria, Prussia, German States and Portugal) versus France, Savoy, Mantua, Cologne and Bavaria; War of the Spanish Succession

1704 British colonial attempts to retake Fort Royal fail

1704 Battle of Blenheim; Malborough defeats French

1706 Battle of Ramillies; French defeat leads to stalemate in Flanders

1707 British colonial attempts to retake Fort Royal fail

1708 Battle of Oudenarde; Marlborough triumphs again

1709 Battle of Malplaquet; Marlborough's most costly and final battle

1710 British capture Port Royal, rename it Annapolis Royal

1711 British expedition against Montreal fails

1713 Treaty of Utrecht; Britain gains Newfoundland and part of Canada

1715 Jacobite Rebellions in Scotland (many exiles settle in North America)

1718 – 1720 War of the Quadruple Alliance (France, Britain, Netherlands and Austria) against Spain

1720 Construction of Louisbourg begins in Nova Scotia; Fortifications on Great Lakes begin

1739 – 1743 "War of Jenkins' Ear"

1740 – 1748 War of the Austrian Succession (King George's War)

1743 Battle of Dettingen (King George II led troops into battle)

1745 Capture of Louisbourg by New Englanders; Battle of Fountenoy; Jacobite Rebellions in Scotland (many exiles settle in North America)

1746 French expedition against Nova Scotia fails; Border raids by French and Indians against Maine

1748 Treaty of Aix-la-Chapelle. Louisbourg returned to France in exchange for Madras

1749 Founding of Halifax.

1754 – 1763 Seven Years War (French and Indian War)

1754 Siege of Fort Necessity; George Washington defeated by French

1755 Braddock's defeat on the Monongahela; Battle of Lake George; "Royal Americans" Light Infantry established; Naval action of Belle Isle; Expulsion of the Acadians

1756 War breaks out in Europe (Prussia and Britain versus France, Austria, Russia and Sweden); Montcalm takes command, captures Oswego

1757 Massacre at Fort William Henry

1758 Amherst and Wolfe seize Louisbourg; Montcalm's victory at Carillon (Ticonderoga)

1759 Capture of Forts Duquesne and Frontenac; British recapture Ticonderoga; Battle of the Plains of Abraham; Battle of Minden

1760 Battle of Ste. Foy; Governor Vaudreuil capitulates, ending French rule in Canada

1763 Treaty of Paris; Britain gains most of North America; Pontiac's Rebellion

Index